Beading
for the first time™

Beading
for the first time™

Ann Benson

Sterling Publishing Co., Inc.
New York
A Sterling/Chapelle Book

Chapelle Ltd.

Owner: Jo Packham

Editor: Leslie Ridenour

Staff: Areta Bingham, Kass Burchett, Marilyn Goff, Holly Hollingsworth, Susan Jorgensen, Barbara Milburn, Linda Orton, Karmen Quinney, Cindy Stoeckl, Gina Swapp, Sara Toliver

Project photography: Kevin Dilley for Hazen Photography

Special Thanks

Thanks to all the fine people at Chapelle Ltd., without whose assistance this book could not have been completed. Thanks also to Carolyn Reese and Ariel Glassman for their help in stitching models for this book.

Library of Congress Cataloging-in-Publication Data

Benson, Ann.
    Beading for the first time / Ann Benson.
        p. cm.
    Includes index.
    ISBN 0-8069-6098-1
    1. Beadwork. I. Title.

    TT860.B64797 2000
    745.58'2--dc21

                                00-048265

10 9 8 7 6 5 4 3 2 1

A Sterling/Chapelle Book

Paperback edition published by
Sterling Publishing Company, Inc.
387 Park Avenue South, New York, NY 10016
© 2001 by Ann Benson
Distributed in Canada by Sterling Publishing
⅝ Canadian Manda Group, One Atlantic Avenue, Suite 105
Toronto, Ontario, Canada M6K 3E7
Distributed in Great Britain and Europe by Cassell PLC
Wellington House, 125 Strand, London WC2R 0BB, England
Distributed in Australia by Capricorn Link (Australia) Pty Ltd.
P.O. Box704, Windsor, NSW 2756, Australia
Printed in China
All Rights Reserved

Sterling ISBN 0-8069-6098-1 Trade
            0-8069-7701-9 Paper

If you have any questions or comments, please contact:

Chapelle Ltd., Inc.
P.O. Box 9252
Ogden, UT 84409
Phone: (801) 621-2777
FAX: (801) 621-2788
e-mail: Chapelle@chapelleltd.com
website: www.chapelleltd.com

For a catalog or more information on products by Ann Benson, please contact:

Ann Benson
P.O. Box 850
Amherst, MA 01004
website: www.annbenson.com

About the Author

Ann Benson is a lifelong resident of New England. She has enjoyed a long and successful career as a designer of beadwork and various needlearts.

She is the author of *Beadweaving*, *Beadwear*, *Beadwork Basics*, and *Two-Hour Beaded Projects* published by Sterling Publishing Co., Inc.

Ann has also enjoyed writing two novels, *The Plague Tales* and *The Burning Road*, published by Delacorte Press. Two more novels are to come.

A mother of two grown daughters, Ann makes her home in Amherst, Massachussetts.

photo courtesy of Bertelsman Publishing

To the Reader

I was once a first-time beader. I am grateful to public librarians throughout New England for procuring the books that made it possible for me to learn beadwork techniques.

It is a challenge to explain the ins and outs of a craft to someone who has never tried it before. In the case of beading, there are many different stitches and techniques, and literally thousands of different styles, colors, and sizes of beads available for use. It is my hope that by exploring this book you will become hooked on beadwork and you will want to try more.

My love of beads grew out of my love for the needlearts in general. However, my greatest devotion is to writing novels. With two already published and two more on the way, I have truly lived my dream. I encourage you to pursue the things you love to do with enthusiasm and pride.

Dedication

In loving memory of Trudy Sandhaus.

Table of Contents

Section 3: Projects Beyond the Basics 64

Beading for the first time

Introduction

The history of the use of beads as decorative accents dates back to pieces found that were used by people of ancient cultures. It spans thousands of years and not only connects every continent, but every civilization of the world.

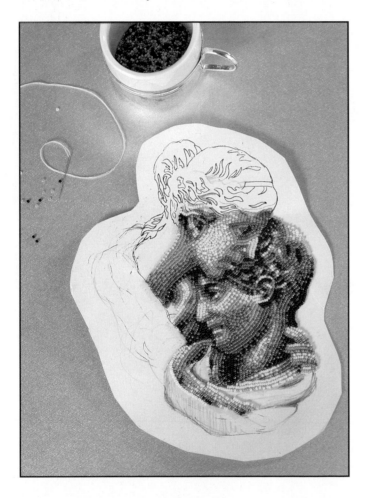

Beads have been in existence since at least 2500 B.C. Examples of beadwork from that era, found at the tombs of Ur, were created with thousands of tiny, fairly consistently sized lapis lazuli beads.

In Egypt, there is evidence that billions of small beads were made for the express purpose of beadwork. As early as 500 B.C., the netted technique, commonly called the "gourd stitch," was developed and used for beadwork, broad collars, funerary jewelry, and mummy nets.

Around 200 B.C., bead manufacturers developed the process of making drawn beads. This formula made possible the production of mass quantities of small, uniformly sized and shaped beads.

The evolution of modern beadwork has been directly influenced by the law of supply and demand. Initially, these drawn beads, known as "Indo-Pacific" beads, were used like currency for the purpose of goods exchange by European explorers who traveled to Africa and Asia.

Similarly, beads were introduced to the Western Hemisphere with the arrival of the European explorers sent to claim and colonize the North and South American continents.

It is assumed that in every case, the traders were successful in exchanging the beads by demonstrating to the native peoples how the beads could be incorporated into other textile arts, such as weaving.

Beads became widely available only after there was interest expressed in incorporating them into already practiced arts and crafts.

Beadwork has evolved over time to satisfy changing fashion trends and desires of the culture. In response to demands for more refined beads, smaller and more colorful beads became available. Subsequently, scale, patterns, and intricacy of workmanship have also changed.

Through various beading techniques and combination of bead types and colors, beadworkers have found the medium to be perfectly suited to artistic expression. Many say they experience a sense of calm and joy while working with the delicate pieces of glass.

How to Use this Book

For the person who is beading for the first time, this book provides a comprehensive guide to supplies, tools, and techniques that can be used to create fabulous decorative and functional beaded objects.

Section 1: Beading Basics familiarizes you with the basic tools and supplies you need to begin beading. Section 2: Techniques contains instructions for eighteen projects that can be made using basic beading techniques. Each technique builds on that which was learned in the previous technique. From gluing to stringing on various fibers, to beading on surfaces, to four different weaving techniques. If you decide to jump ahead out of sequence, you may find you have skipped a technique you now need to use.

Section 3: Projects Beyond the Basics expands on the techniques learned in Section 2 with eleven additional projects that are a bit more complex and sometimes combine two or more techniques, such as a surface-beaded Celtic Knot that becomes a pendant when strings of beads are attached to two sides.

Finally, Section 4: Gallery of Artists presents designs done by artists and professionals in the field. These photographs demonstrate the fabulous effects that can be achieved through the art of beading and will inspire you on to creating your own masterpieces.

The intent of this book is to provide a starting point and teach basic skills. The more you practice beading, the more comfortable you will feel. Allow yourself a reasonable amount of time to complete your first project—remember this is your first time. You will soon discover that the beading techniques are easy to master.

After you have completed the first few projects, you will be surprised by how quickly you will be able to finish the remaining projects. Take pride in the talents you are developing and the unique designs only you can create.

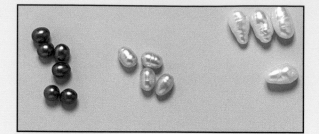
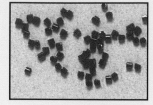

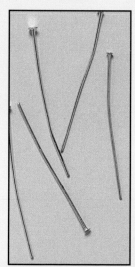

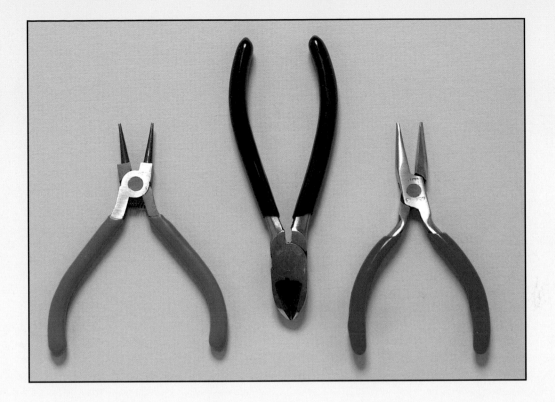

Section 1: *beading basics*

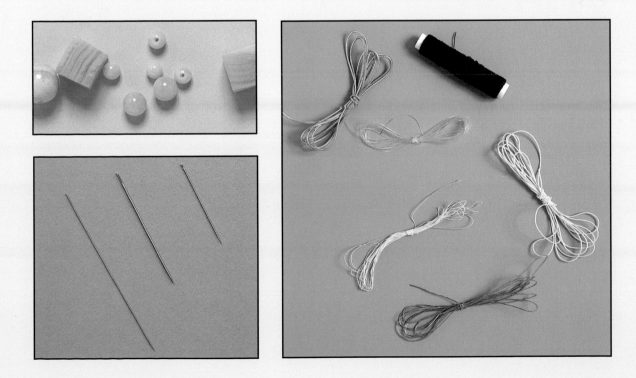

What do I need to get started?

Beads

Seed Beads: Most of us are familiar with these small beads that are often used in traditional Native American jewelry. They are round or oval in shape and have a centered hole.

Seed beads are made of glass that is heated to a molten state. Generally, the beads are colored when metals and other chemicals are infused into the molten mixture. The molten glass is extruded to form beads. When cooled, the beads are sorted for size, from 15/0 (very tiny) to 6/0 (the largest seed bead).

There are no standard packages for beads. Each company that sells beads to an individual consumer has its own put-up size. The following scale may help you determine the number of packages to purchase:

For size 14/0 seed beads:
    1 gram = approximately 200 beads
For size 11/0 seed beads:
    1 gram = approximately 120 beads

Delica Seed Beads: Delica seed beads are also quite small, corresponding roughly to 11/0 seed bead size. The beads are extruded to have a large hole and thin wall, and the shape is tubular. They are excellent for needle-weaving techniques such as the brick stitch on page 56 and the peyote stitch on page 58, because of their consistency in size and shape and because their large holes will accommodate several passes of thread (which is necessary in some weaving techniques). Delicas are readily available in a very wide range of colors and finishes.

Hex Seed Beads: Hex seed beads are six-sided extruded beads with very large holes and very thin walls. They are similar in size to delicas, but the range of colors and finishes is quite a bit more limited. They are also excellent for weaving and are not too difficult to find.

Three-cut Seed Beads: Three-cut seed beads come in two sizes, 12/0 and 9/0. They are literally cut after extrusion to form the flat shiny surfaces that give them a faceted look. The range of colors and finishes is extremely limited, but three-cuts are widely used nevertheless—they are favored on elegant evening clothes because of their extreme sparkle and shine. Note: The holes may be inconsistent, so buy more than you think you will need as a good percentage might be unusable.

Bugle Beads: Bugle beads are long narrow beads with a center hole running the length of the bead. They range from #1 (approximately 2 mm long) to 25 mm (roughly 1"). Occasionally, bugle beads can be found in even longer lengths, but availability is very inconsistent. The most popular sizes to work with are #2 (4 mm), #3 (6 mm), and #5 (12 mm). Generally, bugle beads are used to embellish a design mainly worked in seed beads. Bugle beads work especially well in hand- or loom-woven designs.

Fancy Glass Beads: Available in so many varieties, it is impossible to describe all of the fancy glass beads. Most bead stores and mail-order catalogs will have hundreds of different styles, and most of those styles will come in a range of colors and finishes. Some are merely one color of glass formed into a ball with a beading hole, while others may also incorporate precious metal foils or threads of colored glass.

Faceted Crystal Beads: These cut-crystal beads have a wonderful diamond-like fire when light-struck. They are made of fine quality glass (usually with a high lead content) and are shaped by a mechanized cutting process. They are extremely expensive but readily available.

Cut-crystal beads are available in many shapes and sizes, from 4 mm cone-shaped beads to 18 mm ovals. They are available in a good range of colors (mostly transparent).

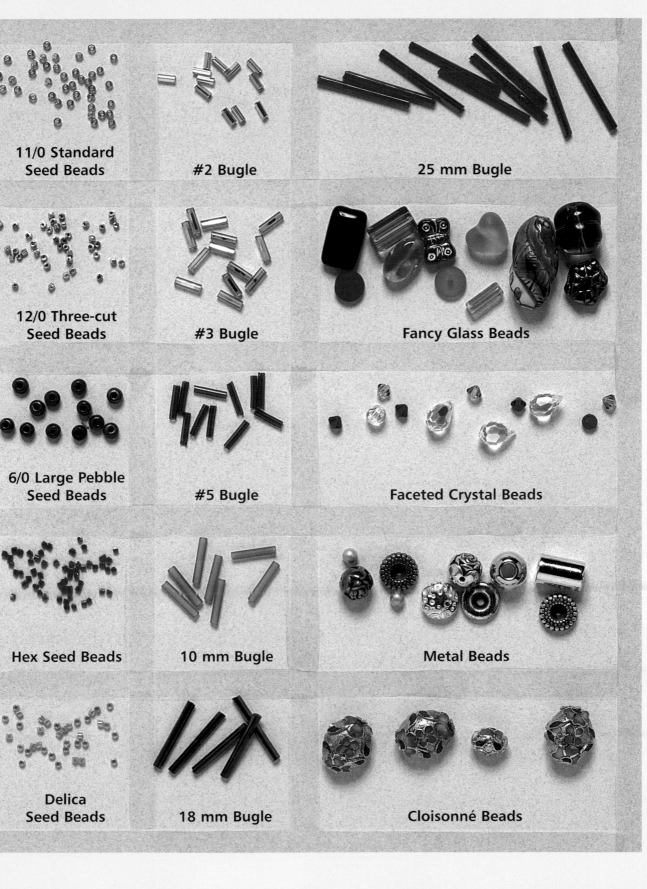

11/0 Standard
Seed Beads

#2 Bugle

25 mm Bugle

12/0 Three-cut
Seed Beads

#3 Bugle

Fancy Glass Beads

6/0 Large Pebble
Seed Beads

#5 Bugle

Faceted Crystal Beads

Hex Seed Beads

10 mm Bugle

Metal Beads

Delica
Seed Beads

18 mm Bugle

Cloisonné Beads

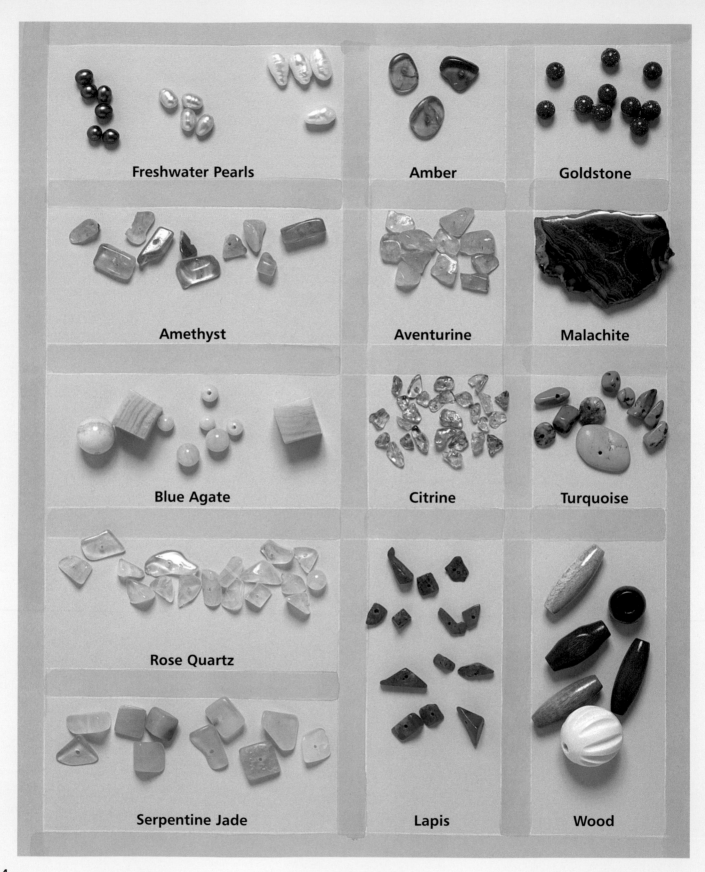

Freshwater Pearls

Amber

Goldstone

Amethyst

Aventurine

Malachite

Blue Agate

Citrine

Turquoise

Rose Quartz

Serpentine Jade

Lapis

Wood

Natural Beads: Natural beads offer a tremendous range of selection. Bone, wood, semiprecious stones—all are easy to find and the choices of color and shape are unlimited. Most bead suppliers carry natural beads (such as turquoise, amethyst, and citrine) in chips of varying grades and finished beads of assorted shapes and sizes.

Most carved beads are made from semiprecious stones; turquoise, amethyst, cinnabar, and some hard quartzes are frequently rendered into recognizable shapes and symbols for use in jewelry-making. Some of the harder semiprecious stones, for instance rose quartz or yellow topaz, are available in faceted shapes. Natural beads are useful in jewelry-making and for embellishing designs that are mainly worked in seed beads.

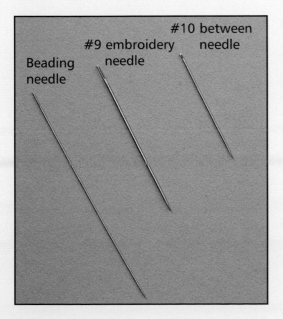

Needles

Needles are essential for almost every technique and project in this book. Make certain to have a good assortment of sharp needles on hand.

Beading needles are traditionally long and thin to accommodate many beads at one time. These needles are particularly useful when stringing strands of beads for bracelets, necklaces, and long fringes. Beading needles are also well suited to weaving on a loom as they can catch several beads at a time when making the return trip on the weft thread.

Traditional beading needles are not well suited for beading on surfaces or needle-weaving. The smaller #9 embroidery needle is ideal when working with seed beads size 11/0 or larger. For some finely drilled stones and pearls, a #10 between needle is recommended.

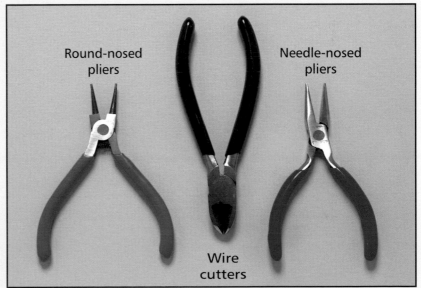

Tools

Several projects require the use of pliers and wire cutters. Round-nosed pliers are used mainly for forming loops in wire eye pins and head pins. Needle-nosed pliers are used for closing loops, flattening and closing crimps, and attaching rings. Wire cutters are used for trimming head pins, eye pins, and beading wire.

You do not have to make a special trip to the craft store to purchase these tools as they are commonly found in most hardware stores. As you become more involved in beading as a needleart, you may require more specialized tools for accomplishing the more difficult techniques. In such case, there are some very fine bead mail-order companies that can accommodate your needs.

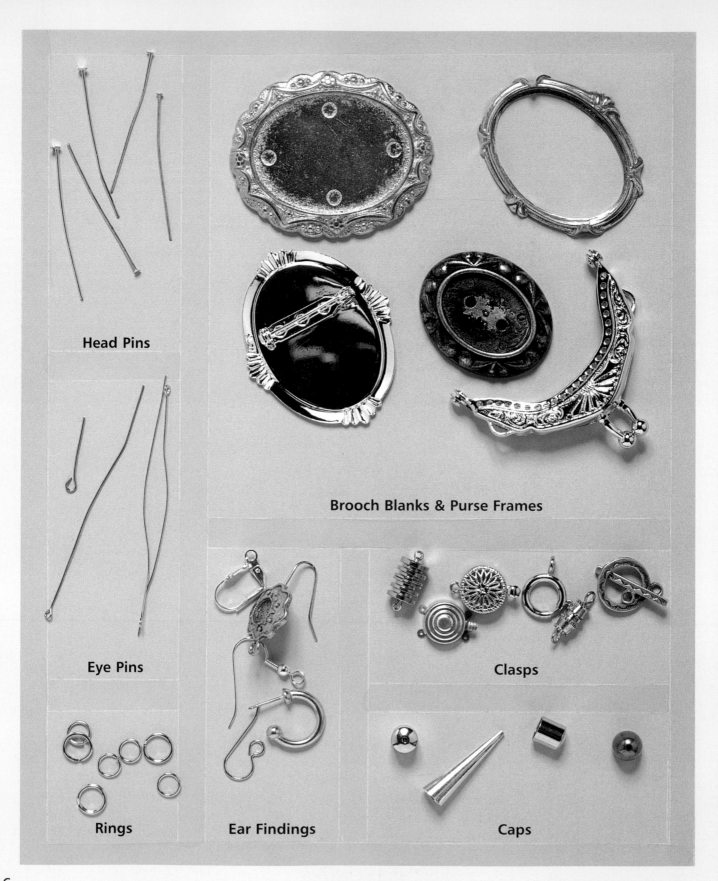

Head Pins

Eye Pins

Rings

Brooch Blanks & Purse Frames

Ear Findings

Clasps

Caps

Jewelry Components

It is easy to make beautiful beaded accessories using jewelry components, also known as "findings." Some strung beadwork (open ended strands, as opposed to continuous loops) will require a component—in most cases, a clasp. Here is an overview of the various sorts of components and their uses:

Head Pins: Head pins are used to attach beads to other types of components such as ear wires and necklace blanks. They are long rigid wires with one end flattened to prevent the bead from slipping off.

Eye Pins: Eye pins are similar to head pins but instead of a flattened end, there is a loop on one end to which a head pin might be attached.

Rings: Rings are often used to attach beads mounted on head pins or eye pins to another component. Rings are also used to form the end of a necklace to which a one-sided clasp such as a claw clasp has been attached. Rings allow free movement of a dropped head pin, which would otherwise be restricted in its movement to one direction.

Brooch Blanks: Brooch blanks are formed metal shapes (some with pin backs already attached) on which beadwork may be mounted. Some blanks that would ordinarily be used to hold a single large cabochon (an oval stone with a flat back, usually of a semiprecious stone such as turquoise or rose quartz) can be used for small pieces of beadwork.

Purse Frames: Purse frames are also made of formed metal and are available in a variety of finishes. These are a very effective type of closure for needle-woven bags.

Ear Findings: Ear findings are available in a wide assortment of styles and types, from simple wires to preformed ear studs with loops for attaching beads. Note: Clip-on earrings are easy to find for those who do not have pierced ears.

Clasps: Clasps are used to close bead strands. Most clasps are two-part metal units that open and close. There are many different types of clasps, some quite decorative; such clasps can become an element of design as opposed to a piece of hardware.

Caps: Caps are used to finish a string or multiple strings of beads. Caps are cylindrical or conical, made of metal, and contain an eye pin. The completed string(s) of beads is knotted onto the eye pin and covered with the cap. The remaining end of the eye pin is then attached to a clasp or ring.

Crimps: Crimps are small tubes of metal that are crushed with pliers or a specific crimping tool to hold wires or cords together. They are useful in attaching clasps to necklaces made of wire.

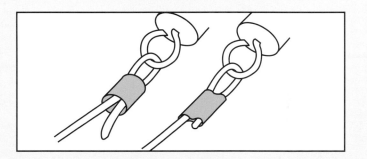

Necklace Blanks: Necklace blanks are generally found in most mail-order catalogs. These can be simple chains or rigid formed wire. Most have clasps already attached, so all you need to do is attach your beads using another component such as a bail or head pin.

Looms

Looms can be very helpful in weaving large (or long) pieces that might otherwise be cumbersome to handle. Good looms can be found in many different sizes and qualities. Some are adjustable to accommodate weaves several inches wide, while others are limited to 2"–3" of width.

All operate on basically the same principle— long or vertical threads (called warp) are placed on the loom and stretched tight. Beads are then attached to these warp threads, using a needle and thread in a horizontal direction, creating weft threads.

The manufacturer of your chosen loom will supply specific directions for attaching warp and finishing the ends of a loomed piece of beadwork. In most cases, the warp can be rolled up at the bottom end so the weave can be quite long. As the work progresses, roll the woven beadwork back and the reserve warp forward.

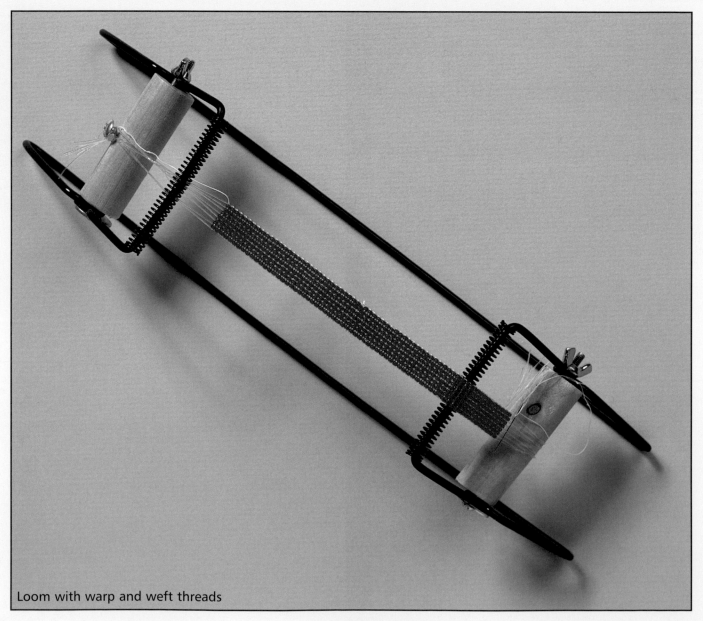

Loom with warp and weft threads

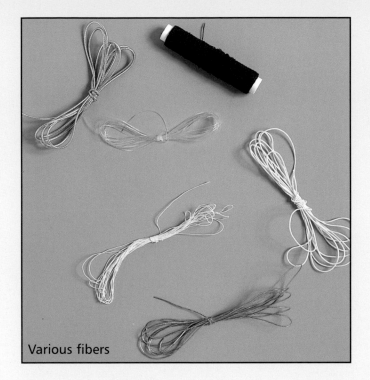
Various fibers

In many cases, the thread or cord will be stiff enough to slip through a bead's hole without the use of a needle. However, lighter weight fibers require the use of a needle. Choosing a needle can be tricky as the eye of the needle must accommodate the thread and still pass through the bead. Another option is to use tape to form a "shoelace" end.

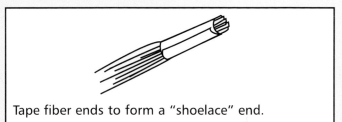
Tape fiber ends to form a "shoelace" end.

Choosing a Fiber

For stringing beads, almost any kind of flexible thread or cord can be used, providing the holes of the beads will accommodate the thread's diameter.

A fiber of an appropriate weight is essential for a nice presentation. For example, very heavy beads must be strung on a substantial fiber, such as elastic, heavy nylon, perle cotton, or multifilament rayon. Nylon monofilament, which is similar to fishing line, is also a good choice for projects with a good deal of weight.

When choosing a fiber, consider the drape of your project. For example, if you are working a necklace and want the necklace to move freely, light silk or nylon, perhaps doubled for strength, is a good choice. But if you want the necklace to take on a defined shape, or to curve predictably, you should use a lightweight twisted wire or nylon monofilament.

For beading on surfaces, needle-weaving, and weaving on a loom, ordinary sewing thread is used most often. A neutral or coordinating color looks best.

Length of Thread

Unless otherwise indicated, cut a 24"–30" length of thread to begin the project. Thread the needle. Slip beads on needle and work beading design, according to project instructions. Note: A longer thread tends to tangle, and a shorter thread necessitates frequent threadings.

Adding a New Length of Thread

When approximately 3" of thread remain unbeaded on the needle and the design is not yet complete, it is time to add a new thread.

Remove the needle from the old thread and cut a new 24"–30" length. Thread the needle, leaving a 5" tail. Tie the end of the old thread and the end of the new thread in a square knot, positioning the knot about 1" from the last bead.

Place a tiny dot of glue on the knot. Wipe off any excess glue and continue beading as if one continuous thread were being used. Note: The glue need not be dry before proceeding.

Allow the thread ends to protrude from the work until the new thread is well established within the design. Pull gently on the knotted ends and clip them close so that they disappear into the design.

Patterns for Beading

For stringing beads, follow individual project instructions for beading order. Many projects include full-color diagrams to help illustrate the written instructions.

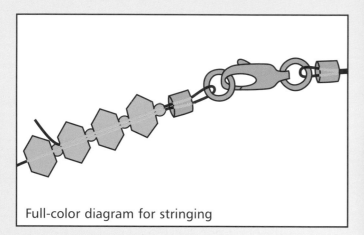

Full-color diagram for stringing

When beading on card stock, the best method for transferring a design is to photocopy it directly onto the card stock.

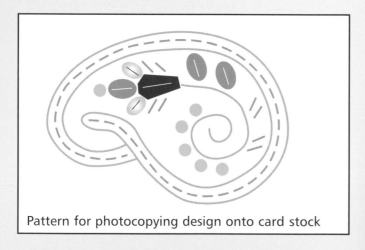

Pattern for photocopying design onto card stock

For beading on fabric, trace the design directly from this book, using a transfer pencil to draw your design onto paper first. Iron the traced design onto the fabric surface. Remember that the design must initially be reversed, or it will come out in mirror image. Another option is to use a light source from underneath. Place the fabric over the design and tape both to a window; trace the design that will emerge as the light shines through.

Beads can be placed to completely cover a design in a printed fabric, or to enhance the printed design.

Beads placed to cover design

An original design can also be sketched directly onto washable fabric using a #2 pencil, which will wash out after one or two launderings. If the sketched design is to be covered entirely in beads, you can use a fine-tipped permanent marker.

Beading on an original sketched design

20

The patterns and color keys provided for squared needle-weaving may remind you of counted cross-stich patterns. One gridded oval represents one bead to be worked into the design. Each colored oval found on the pattern corresponds to a specific size and color of bead, identified on the key which accompanies the pattern.

The pattern is drawn to show vertical rows of beads. Each subsequent row is attached to the previous vertical row by a series of evenly spaced loops of thread. Note: The ideal pattern is to loop after every third bead. In some cases, where great strength is desired, you may want to loop more frequently.

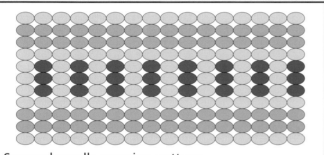

Squared needle-weaving pattern

The patterns and color keys provided for brick stitch needle-weaving and peyote stitch needle-weaving are similar to patterns for squared needle-weaving. However, these patterns are different in that they are drawn to show staggered rows of beads that create a diagonal effect when the design is woven.

The brick stitch causes beads to lie against one another

Brick stitch needle-weaving pattern

horizontally while the peyote stitch causes beads to lie vertically against one another.

For each weaving technique, the rows are initially somewhat unstable and may seem difficult to work. Be patient! After two or three rows, the weaving will be quite easy to handle.

Beading Tips

Spilled Beads: There is no use crying over spilled beads. Instead, put a new bag in your vacuum cleaner and vacuum them up. If only a few beads spilled, wet the tip of your finger to pick them up.

Static Cling: A moistened paper towel reduces the static electricity that builds up around glass beads. Place the wet towel on your flat container while working.

Jumping Beads: If you store your beads in a plastic bag, they will probably try to jump out when you open it. Blow into the bag lightly and the moisture from your breath will settle the beads enough to pour them out.

Counting Beads: It is very tempting when weaving to loop away without recounting your beads after threading on a very long row—but you will only do this once. If you have to remove a row, first pull the needle off the thread. Then use the tip of the needle to gently pull the thread out of the beads.

Organization: Sort beads and place them in small containers with flat, small-lipped lids. A muffin tin also comes in handy as a useful organizer.

Removing Beads: If you accidentally sew on the wrong color or a misshapen bead, or if your work is puckering, remove the offending bead by breaking it off with needle-nosed pliers. Close your eyes and look away as the bead breaks.

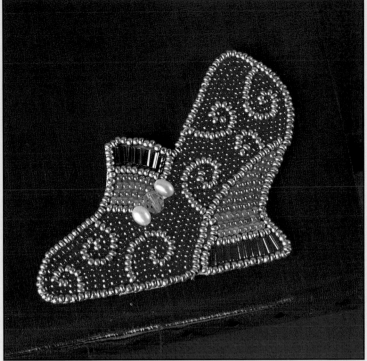

Section 2: *techniques*

How do I use glue to decorate an object with beads?

What You Need to Get Started:

Beads:
#2 and/or #3
   bugle beads:
   light green (300)
11/0 seed beads:
   light green (300)
6/0 seed beads:
   light green (6)

Etc.:
#9 embroidery
   needle
Jewelry glue
Thread: light green
Wooden blank:
   heart-shaped, 1½"

Beads can be glued to most surfaces. Curved or shaped surfaces can present problems when using other beading techniques. However, there are lots of possibilities when beading with glue. This sparkling ornament is created by gluing beads onto all sides of a three-dimensional wooden blank.

Glued Heart Ornament

Here's How:
Note: You will need a clear-drying glue with a strong bond, but one that will allow you some working time. A thirty-minute dry time is ideal.

1. Select beads by comparing bugle beads to one side edge of wooden blank, and choosing size that most closely matches (but is not larger than) width of side edge.

2. Apply glue liberally onto side edge. Using tip of needle, set bugle beads into glue. Allow to dry.

3. Using needle and thread, string beads to desired length for ornament hanger.

4. Glue thread ends of hanger onto back side of wooden blank. Note: You will be working on this side first. Beads will cover thread ends.

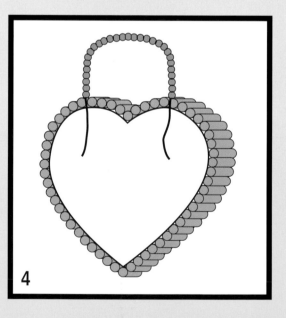

5. Form and glue border of #2 bugle beads around outside edge of back side, adjusting position of beads to accommodate shape.

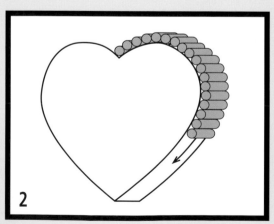

6. Glue three units of four #3 bugle beads around one 6/0 bead. Fill and glue remaining areas with 11/0 seed beads. Allow to dry. Note: Seed beads look better when placed on their sides so holes are not visible, unless flat placement is part of design.

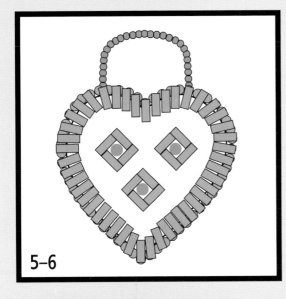

5–6

7. Repeat Steps 5–6 for top side of wooden blank.

Troubleshooting:

To ensure a good grip on the beads, allow the glue to seep into the bead's hole. Do not be afraid to bury the bead in glue. As it dries, the glue will shrink and become clear to reveal the bead.

Avoid glue buildup that may interfere with bead placement by keeping a wet paper towel nearby to clean the tip of your placement tool as needed.

Work in small sections so you can arrange the beads as desired before the glue dries.

When gluing beads on a multisurfaced object, allow each side to dry before going on to the next.

Once the glue dries you cannot go back and shift beads. So do not allow one slightly-out-of-place bead to bother you. Your design does not have to be perfectly symmetrical.

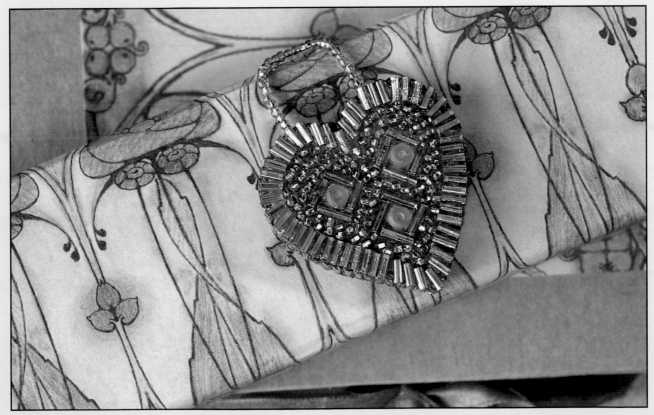

2

technique

How do I string beads on wire?

Beaded wires can be twisted into three-dimensional shapes and used in a variety of ways. This design is made by stringing beads on wires to create three flowers and two leaf clusters, then twisting all wires together to form the napkin ring.

What You Need to Get Started:

Beads:
6 mm x 10 mm amethyst flat beads with hole through length (5)
8 mm blue lace agate round bead
14–16 mm flourite flat beads with hole through center (5)
6 mm rose quartz round bead
11/0 seed beads: dark green; light green; medium green; lavender
4 mm x 13 mm turquoise squared tubes with hole through length (6)

Etc.:
34-gauge beading wire: gold-finished
Wire cutters

Beaded Wire Napkin Ring
Photograph on page 28.

Here's How:

1. Cut twenty-eight 12" lengths of wire.

2. For turquoise flower, slip lavender seed bead on seven wires to middle of length. Fold each wire. Slip blue lace agate bead on one doubled wire. Slip one turquoise squared tube on each remaining doubled wire. Twist remaining length of each wire starting beyond last bead. Position all beaded wires together and twist as one.

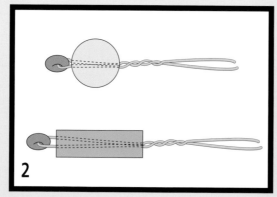

3. For amethyst flower, slip lavender seed bead on six wires to middle of length. Fold each wire. Slip rose quartz bead on one doubled wire. Slip one amethyst flat bead on each remaining doubled wire. Twist remaining length

of each wire starting beyond last bead. Position all beaded wires together and twist as one.

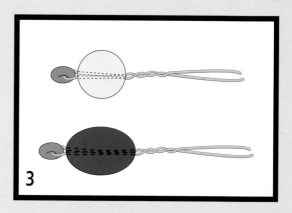

4. For flourite flower, slip three lavender seed beads, one flourite flat bead and three more lavender seed beads on five wires to middle of length. Fold each wire. Twist remaining length of each wire starting beyond last bead. Position all beaded wires together and twist as one.

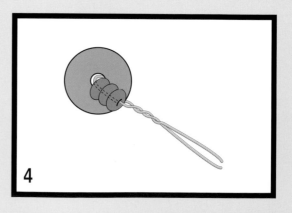

5. For light green leaf, slip one light green seed bead on wire to middle of length. Fold wire. Slip one light green seed bead on doubled wire. Separate wire ends. Slip eleven light green seed beads on each end of wire. Double wire ends again. Slip eight light green seed beads on doubled wire. Twist remaining length of each wire starting beyond last bead.

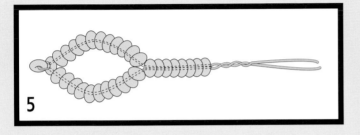

6. For medium green leaf, slip one medium green seed bead on wire to middle of length. Fold wire. Slip one medium green seed bead on doubled wire. Separate wire ends. Slip nine medium green seed beads on each end of wire. Double wire ends again. Slip six medium green seed beads on doubled wire. Twist remaining length of each wire starting beyond last bead. Repeat for second leaf.

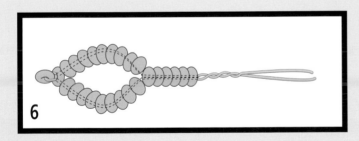

7. For dark green leaf, slip one dark green seed bead on wire to middle of length. Fold wire. Slip one dark green seed bead on doubled wire. Separate wire ends. Slip eight dark green seed beads on each end of wire. Double wire ends again. Slip three dark green seed beads on doubled wire. Twist remaining length of each wire starting beyond last bead. Repeat for second leaf.

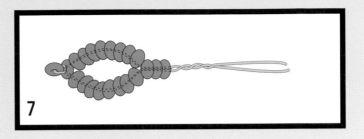

8. Position all leaf wires together, centering light green leaf between two medium green leaves and two dark green leaves, and twist as one.

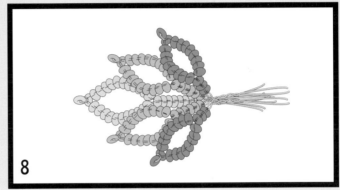

9. For fronds, slip one light green seed bead on wire to middle of length. Fold wire. Slip two light green, one medium green, one light green, two medium green, one dark green, one medium green, and twelve dark green seed beads on doubled wire. Twist remaining length of wire starting beyond last bead. Repeat for five fronds.

10. Position all frond wires together and twist as one.

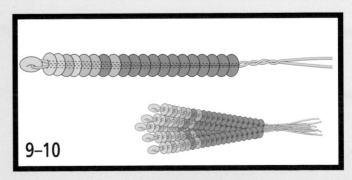

27

11. Position flowers, leaves, and fronds together and twist all wires uniformly to 4" length. Note: Make certain the twist is very tight at the 4" mark.

12. Cut entire twisted group of wires at 4" mark. Bend cut end back ½" to wrap around base of flower spray, forming a ring.

Design Tips:
Use lightweight wire, such as 34 gauge if it is available. Gold-finished wire is pretty enough to be left exposed as part of the design.

Plain metal wire looks dull and should be hidden with a covering of some sort. If you are creating flowers with wire, the twisted wire can be covered with floral tape.

Make certain any visible twisted section of wire has a uniform appearance.

Troubleshooting:
Wire will come off the roll in a spiral shape. Take care to avoid pulling too quickly on this spiral as it will kink. Kinks do not render the wire unusable, but do make it more difficult to position the beads properly if they fall within the design area.

How do I string beads on a head pin jewelry component?

It is easy to make beautiful beaded accessories using jewelry components, also known as "findings." This simple but elegant necklace is created using a preformed necklace blank, two gold beads, one large glass bead, and a head pin.

Rigid Wire Necklace

Here's How:

1. Slip beads on head pin, alternating one gold bead, large glass bead, and then second gold bead.

2. Using wire cutters, trim head pin to ³⁄₁₆" beyond last bead.

3. Using round-nosed pliers, form a loop in end of head pin. Slip loop on wire necklace blank and carefully close loop.

What You Need to Get Started:

Beads:
Glass bead: large
4 mm round
   beads:
   matte gold (2)

Etc.:
Head pin:
   gold-finished,
   .22-diameter,
   2"-long
Round-nosed
   pliers
Wire cutters
Wire necklace
   blank

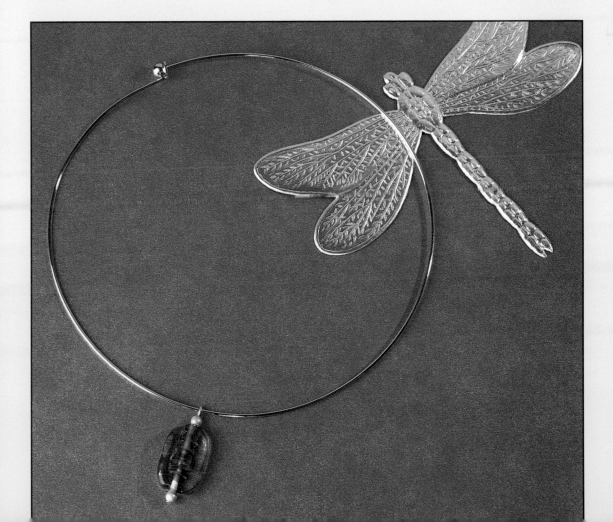

29

4
technique

How do I string beads on multiple jewelry components?

By combining head pin, eye pin, cap, ring, and ear wire components, you can quickly create these attractive earrings.

Faux Pearl Component Earrings

Here's How:
1. Slip teardrop bead and cap on head pin. Slip pearl bead and gold bead on eye pin.

2. Using wire cutters, trim head pin and eye pin to ⅜" beyond cap and gold bead.

3. Using round-nosed pliers, form a loop in end of head pin and eye pin. Slip loop of head pin and eye of eye pin on ring and carefully close each loop. Slip loop of eye pin on ear wire and carefully close loop.

4. Repeat Steps 1–3 for remaining earring.

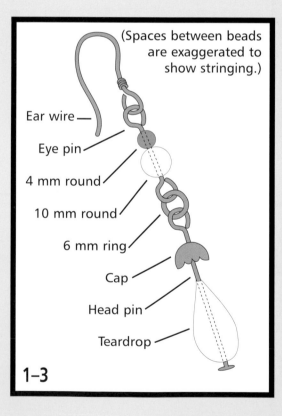

(Spaces between beads are exaggerated to show stringing.)

Ear wire
Eye pin
4 mm round
10 mm round
6 mm ring
Cap
Head pin
Teardrop

1–3

How do I string beads on a needle and thread?

Stringing beads on lighter weight fibers requires the use of a needle. Choosing a needle can be tricky as the eye of the needle must accommodate the thread and still pass through the bead. No clasp is needed to finish this necklace, making it one of the most basic, yet versatile designs in beading.

What You Need to Get Started:

Beads:
Assorted beads

Etc.:
Beading needle
Embroidery scissors
Jewelry glue
Thread, heavy-
    weight: off-white

Continuous Loop Necklace
Photograph on page 32.

Here's How:
Note: Traditional beading needles, which are long and narrow, are excellent for stringing small beads, as they can pick up several beads at a time. Tapestry needles work particularly well when using a heavier weight fiber and larger beads.

1. Cut thread about 6" longer than desired length of necklace. Note: Remember that the finished necklace must be larger than your head—36" is a good length.

2. Thread needle. Slip beads on needle in desired pattern to 36" length.

3. Knot ends together. Apply dot of glue onto knot. Allow to dry.

4. Work excess thread back into bead strand. Loop thread around one bead. Apply dot of glue onto looped thread and pull taut. Repeat looping to secure beads if necessary. Trim excess thread.

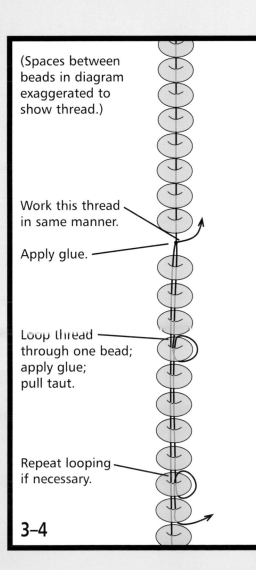

(Spaces between beads in diagram exaggerated to show thread.)

Work this thread in same manner.

Apply glue.

Loop thread through one bead; apply glue; pull taut.

Repeat looping if necessary.

3–4

Design Tips:

Round beads are quite well suited to this type of application, but odd-shaped beads may also be used. If you are using natural stone chips, try to sort them first to avoid using those that have jagged or sharp edges.

Space beads so that each can be shown to its best advantage. A good design method is to place one or several small beads between two larger beads. This is particularly effective when stringing some natural beads which tend to twist unattractively due to their irregular shape.

How do I string beads on elastic?

Elastic thread is available in a variety of weights and colors and should be used where a continuous loop of strung beads must fit closely. Clear elastic thread, which is easy to knot securely, is used to string these multicolored bracelets, which can be worn individually or in a group.

What You Need to Get Started:

<u>Beads</u>:
Assorted beads

<u>Etc.</u>:
Craft scissors
Elastic thread: clear
Jewelry glue

Simple Bracelet

Here's How:
Note: Elastic thread is stiff enough to slip through a bead's hole without the use of a needle.

1. Cut thread about 6" longer than desired length of bracelet. Note: The finished strand length should be your wrist measurement plus 1" before tying. If you are making the bracelet as a gift and do not know the wrist size, 6" is generally a good length when using elastic thread.

2. Slip beads on thread in desired pattern to desired length.

3. Tie two ends together in a simple knot. Apply dot of glue onto knot. Allow to dry.

4. Trim excess thread.

technique

What You Need to Get Started:

Beads:
4–5 mm faceted beads: citrine (75–80)
11/0 seed beads: transparent citrine (75–80)

Etc.:
Claw clasp: gold-finished
Craft scissors
Ear wires: gold-finished (2)
Head pins: gold-finished, .22-diameter, 1½"-long (2)
Monofilament, 8-lb test
Needle-nosed pliers
10 mm ring: gold-finished
Round-nosed pliers
Tube crimps: gold-finished (2)
Wire cutters

How do I string beads on monofilament?

This simple choker is made by stringing faceted citrine beads alternating with glass seed beads. Flexible enough to allow the beads to drape under their own weight, the 8-lb test monofilament used for stringing the beads is also stiff enough to support them.

Faceted Citrine Choker & Earrings

Here's How:
Note: The monofilament is stiff enough to pass through the beads without the use of a needle.

1. Cut one 22" length of monofilament.

2. Knot one end of monofilament to prevent beads from slipping off.

3. Slip beads on monofilament, alternating faceted beads and seed beads to 16" length.

4. Run each end of monofilament through one crimp, one ring on clasp, and back through crimp. Tie a simple knot. Using needle-nosed pliers, flatten crimps over knots. Note: Leave a very small amount of slack in mono-filament (no more than ⅛") when attaching clasp to prevent necklace from being too rigid.

5. Thread excess ends of monofilament back through a few beads on each side and trim close to necklace, taking care to avoid cutting necklace.

6. To make matching earrings, slip beads on gold-toned head pins, alternating faceted beads and seed beads.

7. Using wire cutters, trim each head pin to ⅜" beyond last bead.

8. Using round-nosed pliers, form a loop in end of head pin. Slip loop on ear wire loop and close.

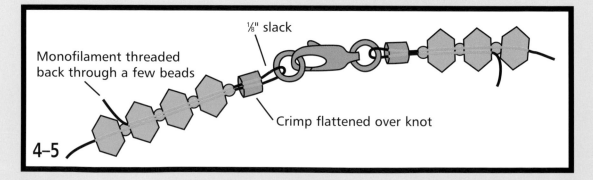

⅛" slack

Monofilament threaded back through a few beads

Crimp flattened over knot

4–5

8
technique

How do I incorporate knotting into stringing beads?

What You Need to Get Started:

Beads:
15 mm amber
  bead
4 mm glass beads
  with large holes
  (70)

Etc.:
Claw clasp: gold-
  finished
Embroidery scissors
Head pin: gold-
  finished,
  .22-diameter,
  2"-long
Jewelry glue
Knotting tool
Needle-nosed
  pliers
Rayon thread,
  lightweight: gold
10 mm ring: gold-
  finished
Sewing needle
Tapestry needle
Wire cutters

Knotting allows you to space beads along a strand and to use a beautiful thread as part of your design.

Knotted Necklace with Amber Bead

Here's How:
1. Cut six 6' lengths of thread. Note: The knots will reduce the length dramatically.

2. Thread tapestry needle with all threads.

3. Slip one glass bead on needle and loosely tie a single knot. Place knotting tool inside loop of knot and gently slide knot close to bead. Continue beading and knotting to 22" length. Note: This is called the "knot sliding technique."

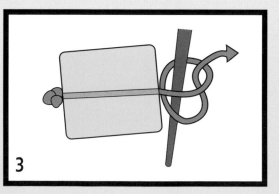

3

4. Knot clasp on one end of length. Knot ring on remaining end.

5. Using sewing needle, sew each thread end back into last few knots on both ends. Apply dot of glue on knots that hold clasp and ring.

6. Slip one glass bead and amber bead on head pin.

7. Using needle-nosed pliers, form loop in end of head pin. Slip loop through center glass bead on knotted strand.

8. Using wire cutters, trim head pin so it can be tucked back into hole of large bead.

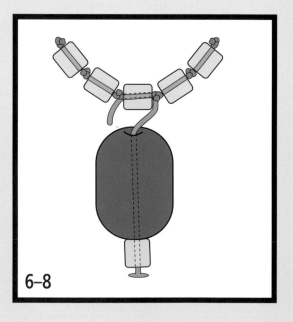

6–8

9. Using needle-nosed pliers, shape head pin and tuck it into hole of large bead.

Design Tips:

Minimize gaps by making certain the knot is made close to the bead.

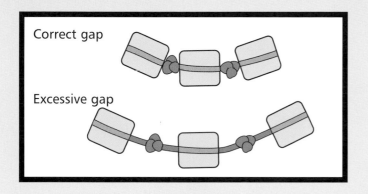

A specific tool can be acquired to help the process of knotting. However there are several common household items that may be used instead, to avoid the cost of an expensive tool. A darning needle, a metal skewer, or the open end of a diaper pin can be used quite effectively.

Troubleshooting:

Avoid using wire or stiff fibers as they are not good choices for knotting.

If your fiber has been wound around a card, it may be kinked. Press out the kinks with a steam iron before knotting to avoid a very crooked strand.

In most cases, there will be a slight crookedness to the strand because the knots will not all be exactly the same size or tautness—this is normal. Steam from a clothing steamer can help to lessen the crookedness. Pull down slightly on the strand to straighten it, then apply steam.

What You Need to Get Started:

Beads:
8 mm round beads with holes large enough to accommodate leather cord: silver (3)

Etc.:
Clasp: silver-finished
Craft scissors
Jewelry glue
Masking tape
Needle-nosed pliers
Pressure crimps: silver-finished (2)
6 mm rings: silver-finished, (2)
Thin leather cords: coordinating colors, 12"-long (3)

How do I use pressure crimps to close a string of beads?

In this design, you will learn to attach pressure crimps. Crimps are used to finish the end of a cord such as leather or rattail so a clasp can be neatly attached. The two open sides of the crimp are flattened over the cord and pressed down tightly. The slight claw at the base of the crimp catches the cord and secures it.

Braided Leather Bracelet

Here's How:
1. Trim cord so ends are neat and unfrayed.

2. Apply dot of glue onto center of pressure crimp. Position three cords, making certain that ends line up. Allow glue to dry. Note: With this type of finding, glue is not absolutely necessary, but it will help to secure the leather even more firmly.

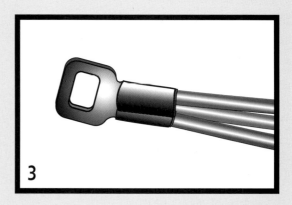

3

4. Tape crimped end of cords to work surface.

5. Braid cords to 3" length, making certain plaits are evenly spaced.

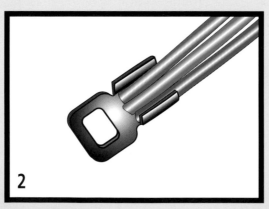

2

3. Using needle-nosed pliers, press one side of crimp down first, then remaining side, until cord is secured.

4–5

6. Slip one bead on each cord and work into braid, adjusting tautness of cord to accommodate beads. Braid cords again to 3" length.

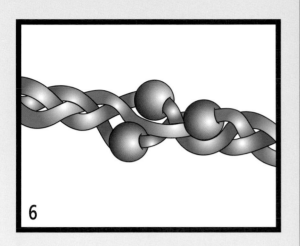

7. Wrap end of braid with small strip of masking tape. Trim cord so ends are even.

8. Repeat Steps 2–3 for cord ends.

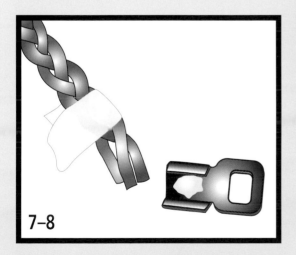

9. Remove tape.

10. Using needle-nosed pliers, attach rings and clasp at both ends.

Design Tips:
Keep the plaits uniform when braiding the leather. Position the beads so the leather settles around them in an attractive manner.

Try using brightly colored leather with large colored beads for a piece of jewelry that has a fun, youthful look.

10
technique

How do I sew beads onto the surface of card stock paper?

What You Need to Get Started:

Beads:
#2 bugle beads:
  lavender (7);
  red (10)
8 mm crystal:
  lavender
6 mm freshwater
  pearls: (2)
11/0 seed beads:
  light aqua (15);
  light blue (15);
  medium blue
  (15); metallic
  gold (250);
  red (350);
  rose (40)

Etc.:
Bath towel: thick,
  white
#10 between
  needle
Card stock: white
Craft scissors
Double-sided
  fusible webbing
#9 embroidery
  needle
Fabric for backing
Iron and ironing
  board
Jewelry glue
Paper: white
Pin back: gold-
  finished, 1¼"
Thread: coordinat-
  ing color

In this project, you will sew beads onto ordinary card stock paper to create an extraordinary piece of jewelry. Card stock is the most desirable weight of paper for use as a beading surface because it is pliable, yet it will also withstand the repeated pull of a needle and thread.

Red Shoe Pin
Photograph on page 43.

Here's How:
1. Photocopy Red Shoe Pin Pattern on opposite page directly onto card stock.

2. Trim the card stock to ½" all around pattern edge, keeping corners somewhat rounded to avoid catching thread.

3. Cut one 30" length of thread and thread needle.

4. Place bugle bead on card stock directly over its photocopied symbol. Bring needle from back of card stock to front at one end of bugle bead. Slip bugle bead on needle and let it slide down thread until it rests on surface. Take needle from front of card stock to back, pulling until bead rests firmly against surface. Note: Bugle beads are almost always sewn on individually.

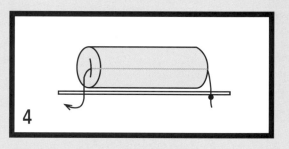

5. Place crystal on surface directly over its photocopied symbol so one cut facet lies flat against surface. Bring needle from back of card stock to front. Slip crystal on needle and let it slide down thread until it rests on surface. Take needle from front of card stock to back at other end of crystal.

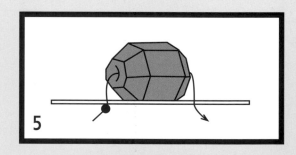

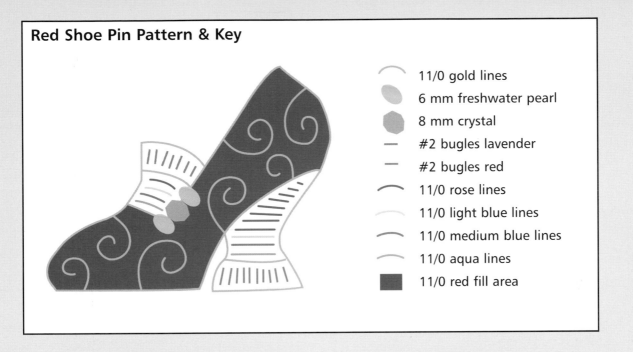

Red Shoe Pin Pattern & Key

- 11/0 gold lines
- 6 mm freshwater pearl
- 8 mm crystal
- #2 bugles lavender
- #2 bugles red
- 11/0 rose lines
- 11/0 light blue lines
- 11/0 medium blue lines
- 11/0 aqua lines
- 11/0 red fill area

6. Since freshwater pearls have extremely fine holes, use #10 between needle and check to see that pearl slips over needle before marking card stock surface for it. Place pearl on surface directly over its photocopied symbol so flatter side lies against surface. Bring needle from back of card stock to front. Slip pearl on needle and let it slide down thread until it rests on surface. Take needle from front of card stock to back at other end of pearl.

7. Sew lines of rose, light aqua, medium blue, and light blue seed beads onto card stock. For each color, bring needle from back of card stock to front at desired starting point. Slip several beads on needle. Lay line against surface and check to see that they comfortably fill desired space. Take needle from front of card stock to back. Secure line using couching technique: returning in direction of starting point, bring needle from back of card stock to front after three beads. Stitch over line, taking needle from front of card stock to back. Repeat for length of line.

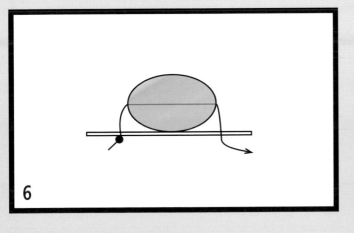

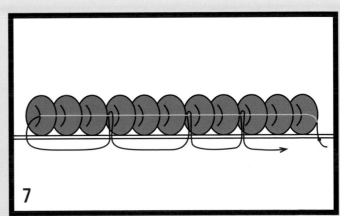

8. For curves and outlines, seed beads may be sewn on two at a time. Bring needle from back of card stock to front about two bead lengths ahead of desired starting point (A). Slip two metallic gold seed beads on needle and let them slide down thread until they rest on their sides on surface. Take needle from front of card stock to back to secure beads (B). Bring needle from back of card stock to front two bead lengths ahead of second bead in line (C). Slip two more beads on needle and let them slide to surface. Take needle from front of card stock to back in first hole made (A). Repeat for length of line.

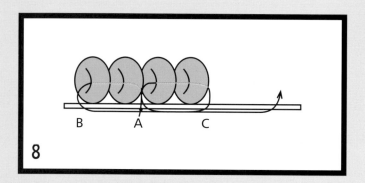

9. Strengthen metallic gold seed bead line with backtracking by bringing needle from back to front just beyond last bead in line and running thread back through all beads in line—run through only three beads at a time, particularly if line is curved. Tighten line until smooth and neat, but not puckering. Take needle from front to back and secure thread. Note: If beads being backtracked have very fine holes, use a #10 between needle.

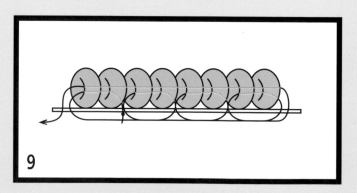

10. Repeat Step 7 with red seed beads to fill in red areas. For small areas and tight curves, sew seed beads onto card stock individually. Bring needle from back of card stock to front at desired starting point. Slip bead on needle and let it slide down thread until it rests on surface. Take needle from front to back through same hole or very close by to secure bead.

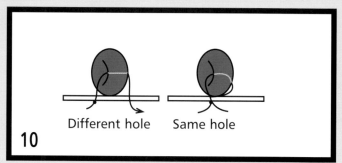

11. To finish back of surface-beaded project, layer and center in order, from bottom: bath towel, beaded card stock wrong side up, fusible webbing with paper removed, backing fabric right side up, and clean white paper. Press iron flat on white paper for five seconds. Shift iron and press for two more seconds to eliminate any steam holes. Allow to cool.

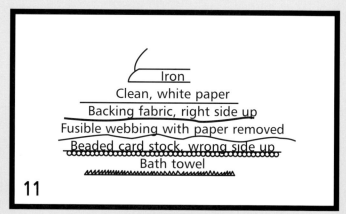

12. Trim excess fabric from edges of beaded project.

13. Apply thin line of diluted glue around trimmed edges to secure.

14. Glue pin back onto back of shoe. Sew through holes on pin back to front of beaded project and secure.

Design Tips:

Ordinary sewing thread is best for beading, and since it is available in a wide array of colors, you can coordinate the color of your thread to the color of your beads.

Each bead will vary a bit in terms of size, so you may not be able to exactly match the placement shown on the card. If you can, try selecting the bead to match the space. If you notice that there are many odd-shaped, flat, narrow, or wide beads, set them aside for possible use when filling in odd-shaped spaces.

Troubleshooting:

If you want to trace a design, a good way to do that is to use a light source from underneath. Place your card stock over the design and tape both to a window; trace the design that will emerge as the light shines through. You may also use a transfer pencil to draw your design first, then iron it onto the surface. Remember that the design must initially be reversed, or it will come out in mirror image.

When trimming excess fabric or paper from the beaded design, take care not to accidentally cut a long string of beads near the edge.

For additional threadings, refer to Adding a New Length of Thread on page 19.

How do I sew beads onto the surface of fabric?

Fabric is the most widely used surface for beadwork. The best fabrics to use are those that have a tight weave but also have some substance. This project is created using a purchased shirt and surface-beading techniques.

Collar Adornment
Photograph on page 46.

Here's How:
1. Using transfer pencil, trace Collar Adornment Pattern on opposite page onto white paper first. Iron design onto collar points. Note: Initially, reverse design or it will come out in mirror image.

2. Cut one 30" length of thread and thread needle.

3. Beginning with large lower flower, position turquoise chip on collar. Bring needle from back of collar to front and slip chip on needle, letting it slide down thread until it rests flat against collar. Slip one turquoise seed bead on needle and take needle back through hole in chip. Pull thread taut until seed bead acts as an anchor on surface of chip, forming flower center.

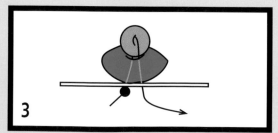

4. Sew nine pearls around turquoise chip to form flower.

5. Sew three light blue and three light green bugle beads on opposite sides of flower to form leaf clusters.

6. Repeat Step 3 for jade chip with medium green seed bead.

7. Work stems in medium green seed beads toward remaining flowers. Run backtracking thread through beads to stabilize curves.

8. Repeat Step 3 at stem indicated for amethyst flat bead with pink seed bead.

9. Sew thirteen light blue bugle beads around amethyst bead to form flower.

10. Sew three light green bugle beads on side of flower to form leaf clusters.

11. Repeat Step 6.

12. Repeat Step 7 for short stem.

13. Sew one pearl at stem indicated to form flower center.

14. Repeat Step 3 for six light pink 6/0 beads with pink seed beads around pearl to form flower.

15. Repeat Step 10.

16. Repeat Step 7 for two remaining stems.

17. Repeat Step 3 at stem indicated.

18. Repeat Step 3 for two light pink 6/0 beads with pink seed beads.

19. Repeat Step 5.

Design Tips:

Select a garment that has a pointed collar and is made of a tightly woven fabric. Knit fabrics are not suitable.

Choose any color of fabric that coordinates with the beads you have chosen.

A garment that has been beaded may be hand-washed and line-dried after beading.

If a very lightweight fabric such as silk, satin, or taffeta is used for beadwork, a backing such as cotton broadcloth or lightweight felt should be fused onto the fabric to stabilize it. Following manufacturer's instructions, use lightweight fusible webbing to adhere a backing onto project fabric before beading.

When using a hoop to stabilize fabrics, make certain that the entire area to be beaded fits within the hoop. Once beads are sewn onto the fabric, it cannot be shifted, as the beads will get in the way of the hoop.

Troubleshooting:

For additional threadings, refer to Adding a New Length of Thread on page 19.

Collar Adornment Pattern & Key

#2 bugles light blue
#2 bugles light green
11/0 medium green lines
4–5 mm freshwater pearl
6/0 light pink
12 mm amethyst
turquoise chip
light jade chip

How do I sew beads onto the surface of needlepoint canvas?

Just as in regular needlepoint, where one stitch is formed over the intersection of two canvas threads, beads are sewn individually to the intersection of two canvas threads. The appearance of the finished work is quite similar to needlepoint because each bead is approximately the same size and shape as a traditional half-cross stitch.

What You Need to Get Started:

Beads:
#2 bugle beads: silver-lined gold (50)
14/0 seed beads: cream (5); dark green (100); metallic gold (75); light green (75); medium green (100); medium pink (35); pale pink (6); red (40)

Etc.:
#10 between needle
Embroidery scissors
Felt for backing: dark green, 4" square
#18 interlock needlepoint canvas: 3" square
Jewelry glue
Masking tape
Satin ribbon, ⅛"-wide: red, 8"-long (2)
Steam iron and ironing board
Threads: dark green; off-white

Holly Heart Ornament
Photograph on page 49.

Here's How:
Note: Experienced needlepointers will notice that the thread is running in a different direction. In order to make the bead slant to the right, the thread must slant to the left. Additionally, the fine embroidery or between needle required will feel very tiny to a stitcher accustomed to the firm bulk of a tapestry needle.

1. Tape edges of needlepoint canvas.

2. Cut one 60" length of off-white thread. Double thread on needle and knot thread ends.

3. Following Holly Heart Ornament Pattern on page 48, work one horizontal row at a time for uniform appearance—from right in short backstitches or from left in long backstitches. Bring needle up from back of canvas (A). Slip one bead on needle and take needle to back of canvas (B). Bring needle

Short Backstitch

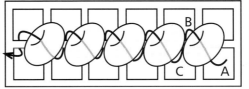

Long Backstitch

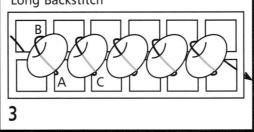

3

from back of canvas (C). Secure thread by holding it against back of canvas and stitching over it with first few beads. Continue in this manner to end of horizontal row. Start next row and return in opposite direction using appropriate stitch. Note: Mark off each row on the graph after completion, as it will help you keep track of your place.

4. Trim canvas to ¼" around design. Clip curves as shown and turn under. Using steam iron, press clipped edges flat so canvas does not show on beaded side of piece.

Pressed flat, trimmed, and clipped

4

5. Using pressed beadwork as template, cut two pieces of felt to size and shape. Trim one piece of felt ⅛" all around for padding.

6. Sew one piece of ribbon to wrong side of beaded canvas at each curve of heart.

7. Sandwich padding felt between wrong side of beaded canvas and backing felt. Using needle and dark green thread, slip-stitch backing felt to beaded canvas, enclosing padding felt and ribbons ends.

8. Sew a row of bugle beads all around edge of heart-shaped ornament. When bugle beads are in place, backtrack through all the bugle beads to position

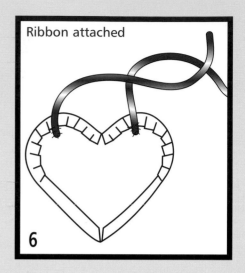

Ribbon attached

6

them more firmly. Bury excess thread in ornament and trim it close.

9. Tie ribbon ends in bow and trim as needed. Note: A dot of glue on the knot will help keep the bow intact when hanging it.

Design Tips:

Use 11/0 seed beads on 14-count canvas. Use 14/0 seed beads on 18-count canvas.

If possible, paint the design on the canvas before beading, following your stitching chart.

Troubleshooting:

Use interlock (single thread lock-weave) canvas or Penelope (double-threaded canvas). Mono (single thread overweave) canvas is too unstable for use with beads.

For additional threadings, refer to Adding a New Length of Thread on page 19.

Holly Heart Ornament Pattern & Key

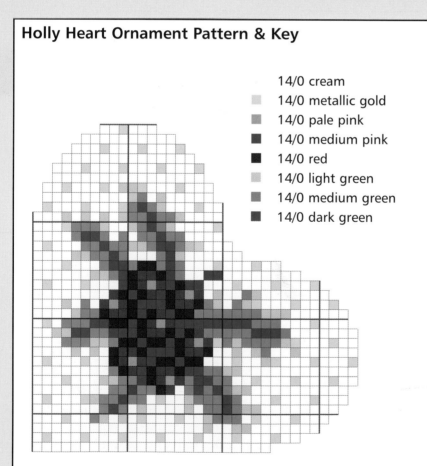

14/0 cream
14/0 metallic gold
14/0 pale pink
14/0 medium pink
14/0 red
14/0 light green
14/0 medium green
14/0 dark green

How do I weave beads on wire?

Weaving is the process of forming a design piece by interlacing multiple beads. A quick yet elegant decorative accent, this purchased tassel is embellished with a band of bugle beads woven on 34-gauge beading wire.

What You Need to Get Started:

<u>Beads</u>:
#5 bugle beads: color to match tassel (22 for ½" diameter)

<u>Etc.</u>:
34-gauge beading wire: 24"-long
Purchased tassel
Wire cutters

Bugle-beaded Tassel

Here's How:
1. Slip one bugle bead on wire to center of length.

2. Slip another bugle bead on either end of wire, then insert remaining end into opposite end of bugle bead. Pull wire taut.

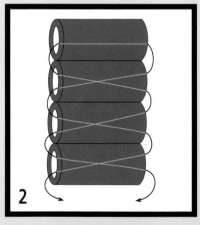

3. Repeat Step 2 to make a length of bugle beads that fits around wrapped section of tassel.

4. To join length into a circle around tassel, insert working end of wire through first bugle bead on length. Twist wires together until secure.

5. Using wire cutters, trim twisted wires to ½". Bury wires in tassel.

Design Tips:
Children old enough to handle wire safely can make little rings and bracelets using this technique.

How do I weave a daisy chain using a needle?

This hand-weaving technique uses a single needle to create a pretty strand that looks as if it is made up of tiny flowers. When worked entirely in one color, it has a lacy look; when worked in multiple colors as in our anklet, the flowery look emerges.

Daisy Chain Anklet
Photograph on page 52.

Here's How:
Note: Each unit of the chain is composed of nine beads, eight "petals" of the same color in a circle around one "center" of a different color.

1. Cut one 24"–30" length of thread. Note: Additional lengths of thread can be added if necessary. The finished anklet length is 9¼".

2. Thread needle, allowing long thread end at beginning of weave. Note: You may tape the end of the beginning thread to a flat surface for stability.

3. Slip eight beads of first color on needle. Run needle back through first bead on thread as shown in diagram. Slip red bead on for "center." Then run needle through lower left bead of circle of eight.

4. Slip one bead of second color on needle. Run needle through lower right bead of first "flower." Slip one more bead on needle and run needle through first bead of second color.

Slip six more beads on needle. Slip red bead on for "center." Then run needle through lower left bead of circle of eight.

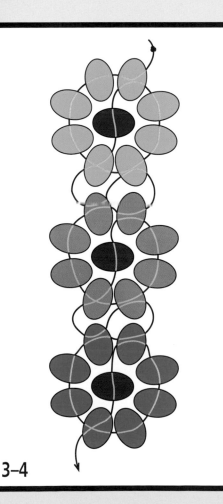

3–4

What You Need to Get Started:

Beads:
11/0 seed beads: light blue (32); gold (24); light green (32); medium green (24); lavender (32); orange (24); light pink (32); red (31); turquoise (24); yellow (24)

Etc.:
Claw clasp: silver-finished
Embroidery scissors
10 mm ring: silver-finished
Sewing needle
Thread: off-white

5. Repeat Step 4 for thirty-one flowers—each one a different color than previous.

6. Run thread through lower left bead of last flower.

7. Sew clasp on one end of length and ring on remaining end, running thread through adjacent beads three times.

8. Bury thread ends in weave by running each thread end back into last bead.

9. Trim excess thread, taking care to avoid cutting weave threads.

Troubleshooting:

For additional threadings, refer to Adding a New Length of Thread on page 19.

How do I create a beaded design using squared needle-weaving?

The technique used for basic needle-weaving is similar to that of crocheting. After the first row is worked, subsequent rows are looped into the first row in a predictable way. Unlike crochet, which is usually worked from written instructions, bead needle-weaving is worked from a gridded pattern. Each of these candleholders is decorated with a needle-woven band of beads.

Wrapped Candleholder
Photograph on page 55.

Here's How:
Note: Bead amounts will depend on how long each band must be woven to wrap around the candleholder you choose.

1. Cut one 30" length of thread and thread needle, leaving 5" tail.

2. To keep design pattern beads from slipping off thread, create "stopper bead." Slip one bead on needle and let it slide down thread to 3" from end of thread. Loop thread back through bead and pull taut. Secure stopper bead to flat or slightly curved surface to stabilize thread. Note: The stopper bead will be removed after the first few rows.

3. Following Wrapped Candleholder Pattern on page 54, string beads for Row 1 from top to bottom. Skipping last bead, insert needle back through all beads. Note: The needle should emerge from the top bead of Row 1.

What You Need to Get Started:

Beads:
11/0 seed beads: dark blue; light blue; metallic gold; lavender

Etc.:
Candleholder with round shaft
Embroidery scissors
Sewing needle
Thread: off-white

2–3

53

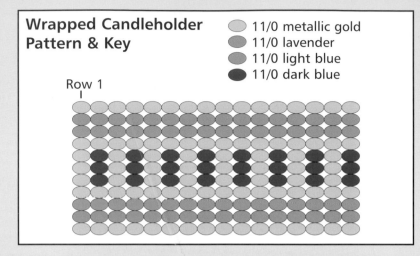

Wrapped Candleholder Pattern & Key

- 11/0 metallic gold
- 11/0 lavender
- 11/0 light blue
- 11/0 dark blue

Row 1

4. String beads for Row 2, from top to bottom. Insert needle into loop exposed at bottom of Row 1. Pull thread gently until entire second row is taut, but not tight, and beads rest against first row without puckering. Note: The work in needle-weaving always proceeds in the direction of the beadworker's dominant hand.

5. Insert needle into last bead of Row 2, and bring thread out until it is taut, but not tight. Loop thread around Row 1 so it is nestled between beads 11 and 10 of Row 1. Insert needle into beads 10 and 9 of Row 2, bringing needle out between beads 9 and 8 on Row 2. Again, thread should be taut, but not tight.

6. Loop thread around Row 1 so it is nestled between beads 9 and 8 of Row 1. Insert needle into next three beads on Row 2—beads 8, 7, and 6—bringing needle out between beads 6 and 5 on Row 2. Tighten thread again.

7. Loop it around Row 1 so it is nestled between beads 6 and 5 of Row 1. Insert needle into next three beads on Row 2—beads 5, 4, and 3—and repeat looping and inserting process until thread emerges from bead 1 of Row 2.

8. Repeat Steps 4–7 for all subsequent rows until band is long enough to wrap snugly around candleholder. Note: The weaving gets easier to handle as the design grows.

9. When about 3" of thread remains unbeaded on needle, it is time to add new thread. Remove needle from thread and cut new 30" length. Thread needle, leaving 5" tail. Note: A longer thread tends to tangle, and a shorter thread necessitates frequent threadings.

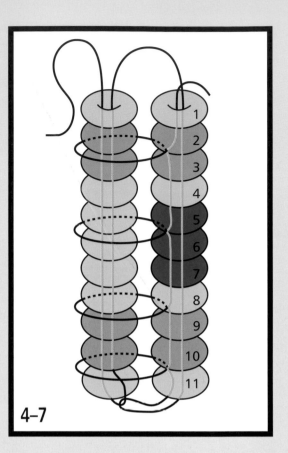

4–7

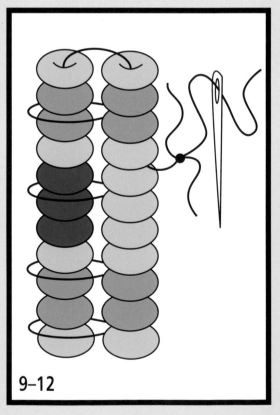

9–12

10. Tie a square knot so that knot lands 1" from where old thread emerges from bead-work.

11. Place tiny dot of glue on knot. Wipe off any excess glue. Note: The glue need not be dry before proceeding.

12. Continue beading as if one continuous thread were being used. Allow thread ends to protrude from work until new thread is well established within weave.

13. Pull gently on thread ends and clip them close so they disappear into woven design. Note: It might be necessary to use a smaller needle until the area of the knot has been passed.

14. Trim any excess threads that occur in body of weave.

15. Wrap length of woven band around candleholder, lining up beads of last row next to beads of Row 1.

16. Repeat Steps 4–7, treating last row as if it were Row 1 and Row 1 as if it were Row 2.

17. Bury excess thread in weave.

How do I create a beaded design using brick stitch needle-weaving?

The brick stitch is a diagonal weaving technique worked in hand using two needles. All work progresses outward from a central foundation row. In this technique the beads lie horizontally against one another like alternating bricks. The resulting weave is strong and flexible, and can be used for many different purposes.

Brick Stitch Barrette

Here's How:
1. Cut one 24" length of thread, and thread each end onto a needle.

2. Following Brick Stitch Barrette Pattern on opposite page, slip first seed bead of foundation row on one needle and let it slide down thread to center. Slip second seed bead on one needle and weave second needle through opposite hole in bead. Pull thread taut, but not tight so beads rest against each other. Continue in this manner to form foundation row.

3. To minimize tangling, remove needle from thread end that will work rows above foundation row.

4. Working in opposite direction, slip one bead on remaining needle at a time and loop thread back into foundation row to end of second row. Note: Beginning with the second row, each row will have one less or one more bead than the previous row.

5. Returning in opposite direction, slip one bead on needle at a time, and loop thread back into second row to end of third row, forming diagonal weave.

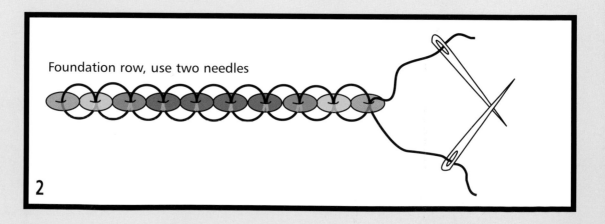

Foundation row, use two needles

2

6. Repeat Step 5 for remaining rows below foundation row. Remove needle from thread.

7. Rethread remaining thread onto needle. Rotate work piece 180° and repeat Steps 4–6 for rows above foundation row.

8. Bury excess threads in weave.

9. Apply glue onto back of woven piece. Center and place woven piece on barrette. Using paper towel, wipe any excess glue from edges of woven piece. Note: Do not be concerned about glue that may seep up through the weave as it will dry clear.

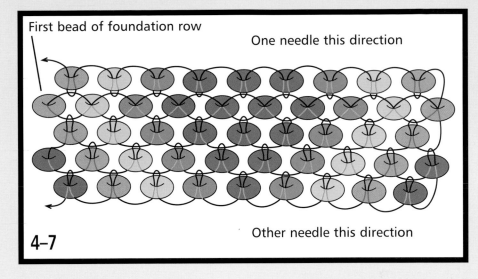

First bead of foundation row

One needle this direction

Other needle this direction

4-7

Design Tip:
Delica beads also work particularly well when using the brick stitch.

Troubleshooting:
For additional threadings, refer to Adding a New Length of Thread on page 19.

Brick Stitch Barrette Pattern & Key

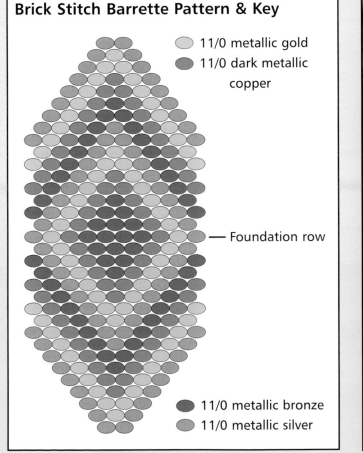

○ 11/0 metallic gold

● 11/0 dark metallic copper

— Foundation row

● 11/0 metallic bronze

○ 11/0 metallic silver

How do I create a beaded design using peyote stitch needle-weaving?

Beads:
11/0 seed beads:
  powder blue
  (11); coral (12);
  metallic gold
  (250); lime green
  (11); orange (8);
  purple (450);
  rose (11);
  turquoise (11);
  lemon yellow (12)

Etc.:
Beading needle:
  small
Embroidery flosses:
  blue; coral; gold;
  lime green;
  turquoise
Embroidery scissors
Masking tape
Sewing needle:
  medium
Thread: off-white

The peyote stitch is a weaving technique worked in hand using a single needle. The weave causes the beads to lie vertically against one another in a staggered pattern. It is very flexible and can be used flat or adapted into three-dimensional shapes. It is easy and pleasurable to do and works up quickly.

Peyote Stitch Bookmark
Photograph on page 60.

Here's How:
Note: Unlike squared needle-weaving where the beads are in neat horizontal and vertical rows, the peyote stitch creates a diagonal effect. The beads that begin and end each row will not be directly above or below the beginning and ending beads of the adjacent rows. At first this may be somewhat confusing, but if you follow the pattern consistently, the weave will stabilize after a few rows.

1. Cut one 24" length of thread and thread needle.

2. Following Peyote Stitch Bookmark Pattern on opposite page, slip beads for top two rows and first bead of third row—beads 1–15—on beading needle at same time, leaving 3"–4" of thread at end. Note: Try to select beads with especially large holes for the top and bottom rows as they will accommodate the floss fringe.

3. Tape thread end onto flat surface for stability.

4. Run needle through bead 13, slip bead 16 on needle and run needle through bead 11. Continue in this manner to end of row.

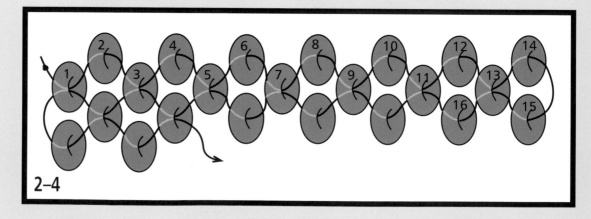

2–4

5. Turn work at end of row to be able to proceed with weave in direction of your dominant hand.

6. Continue working each individual bead between two beads of previous row.

7. When weave is complete, bury thread end within weave. Trim thread end.

8. Thread sewing needle with turquoise embroidery floss. Double floss and run through first bead in top row. Knot fringe close to bead and trim fringe length to 4". Repeat for remaining beads and floss in following order: blue, lime green, turquoise, gold, coral, and turquoise.

9. Rotate bookmark 180° and repeat Step 7 for fringe on bottom row.

Design Tips:

For this design, choose beads with particularly large holes, as you will be working a double strand of embroidery floss through the holes of the top and bottom rows to create a fringe.

The peyote stitch can be used to create very wide weaves for use in larger beaded items such as handbags, and can be worked around shapes such as tubes and cylinders.

Troubleshooting:

Take care when turning at the end of each row to keep the tension of your thread consistent so that the edge is neat.

For additional threadings, refer to Adding a New Length of Thread on page 19. Try to work it so the knot of the new thread lands in the center of a row to avoid a lumpy-looking edge.

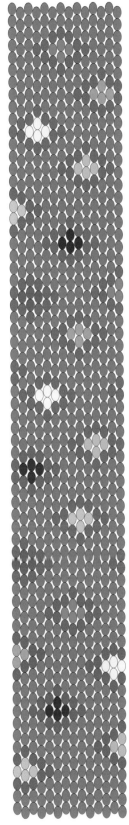

Peyote Stitch Bookmark Pattern & Key

- ○ 11/0 lemon yellow
- ● 11/0 metallic gold
- ● 11/0 orange
- ● 11/0 coral
- ● 11/0 rose
- ● 11/0 purple
- ● 11/0 powder blue
- ● 11/0 turquoise
- ● 11/0 lime green

How do I weave a beaded design using a loom?

Looms are excellent for weaving large (or long) beaded pieces that might otherwise be cumbersome to handle. Long vertical threads (called warp) are placed on the loom and stretched tight. Beads are then attached to these warp threads using a needle and thread in a horizontal direction.

Loom-woven Band
Photograph on page 63.

Here's How:
1. Following manufacturer's instructions, warp loom with ten warp threads. Note: In any loomed piece the warp will have one more thread than the number of beads across the width of the design.

2. Cut one 30" length of thread and thread needle. To start horizontal (or weft) thread, knot end of thread onto left outermost warp thread. Note: Make certain to knot the thread onto the right outermost warp thread if you are left handed.

3. Following Loom-woven Band Pattern on page 62, slip beads for top horizontal row on needle.

4. Pass beaded thread under warp threads, positioning beads and threads so one bead falls between two warp threads.

5. After beads are seated into warp, pass needle back through beads so weft thread goes over warp threads.

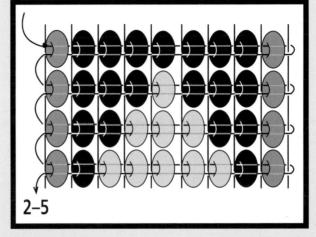

2–5

What You Need to Get Started:

Beads:
11/0 seed beads:
   black; light blue;
   medium blue;
   gold; light green;
   lime green;
   medium green;
   lavender; orange;
   pink; turquoise;
   yellow

Etc.:
Beading loom
Beading needle
Embroidery scissors
Thread: off-white

6. Repeat Steps 3–5 for remaining horizontal rows.

7. Bury any excess thread in weave.

8. To finish ends of band, separate warp threads into groups of two threads, beginning from each side of center weft bead. Note: Outermost warp threads will remain single.

9. Trim each group of threads as one for a clean edge. Thread #9 embroidery needle with these threads.

10. Slip twelve black and one of each remaining color (in order of rainbow) 11/0 seed beads on needle.

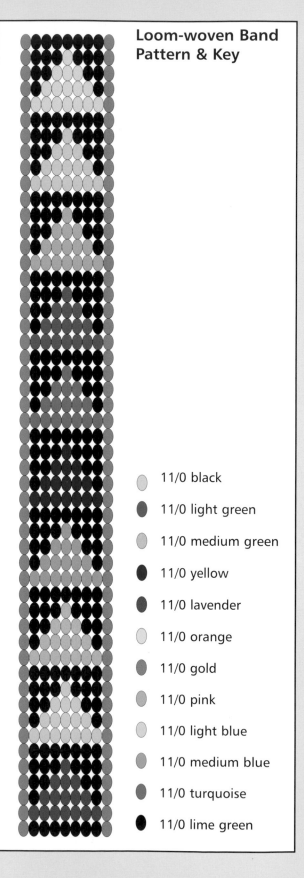

Loom-woven Band Pattern & Key

- ○ 11/0 black
- ● 11/0 light green
- ○ 11/0 medium green
- ● 11/0 yellow
- ● 11/0 lavender
- ○ 11/0 orange
- ● 11/0 gold
- ○ 11/0 pink
- ○ 11/0 light blue
- ○ 11/0 medium blue
- ● 11/0 turquoise
- ● 11/0 lime green

11. Knot threads, positioning beads very close to woven band. Note: It may be necessary to knot over the first knot one or more times to make certain that the beads are secure.

Alternate Design Patterns & Keys

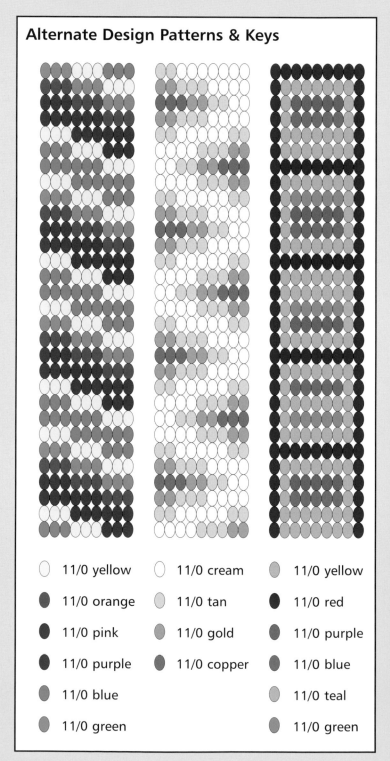

- ○ 11/0 yellow
- ● 11/0 orange
- ● 11/0 pink
- ● 11/0 purple
- ● 11/0 blue
- ● 11/0 green

- ○ 11/0 cream
- ○ 11/0 tan
- ● 11/0 gold
- ● 11/0 copper

- ○ 11/0 yellow
- ● 11/0 red
- ● 11/0 purple
- ● 11/0 blue
- ○ 11/0 teal
- ● 11/0 green

12. Apply small dot of glue on knot. Trim excess thread.

13. Repeat Step 10 for each remaining warp thread. Skipping last bead, insert needle back through all beads. Bury excess thread in weave.

Troubleshooting:

For additional threadings, refer to Adding a New Length of Thread on page 19.

Section 3: *projects beyond the basics*

1
project

What You Need to Get Started:

Beads:
#2 bugle beads:
  matte purple;
  matte magenta
#3 bugle beads:
  amber; coral
#5 bugle beads:
  matte blue;
  metallic gold
11/0 seed beads:
  light blue;
  medium blue;
  coral; cream;
  dark green;
  light green;
  medium green;
  lavender; metallic
  lavender; peach;
  pink; matte
  purple; metallic
  purple; dark
  purple
6/0 seed beads:
  amber; light
  green; medium
  green

Etc.:
Craft knife
#9 embroidery
  needle
Jewelry glue
Wooden box: oval-
  shaped, 2½" x 3½"

How do I use artwork as a pattern for gluing beads?

Design resources are plentiful for glued beading. Here, a greeting card, cut to fit onto the top of an oval-shaped box, serves as the pattern for bead placement.

Glued House Box

Here's How:

1. Color-photocopy House Artwork onto paper.

2. Glue copied design onto top of box lid. Trim paper around lid.

3. Select beads by comparing elements in copied design and choosing size and color that most closely matches.

4. Apply glue liberally onto printed surface of card, covering one section of lid. Using tip of needle, set beads of corresponding size and color into glue. Allow to dry.

5. Repeat Steps 3–4 for next section to be beaded.

Design Tip:

Try using a photograph in this manner. Or, sketch your own design directly onto a surface and bead within the outline of the design.

House Artwork

2
project

What You Need to Get Started:

<u>Beads</u>:
11/0 seed beads:
  black; light
  green; medium
  green; light pink;
  pink; medium
  rose

<u>Etc.</u>:
Acrylic paint:
  burgundy
26-gauge beading
  wire: tinned
  copper-finished
Fabric: gold/teal,
  2" x 20"
Florist tape: olive
  green
Needle-nosed pliers
Paintbrush
Pin back: silver-
  finished, 1¼"
Sewing needle
Thread: teal
Velvet leaves:
  olive green,
  large (2)
Wire cutters

How do I form complex shapes with wire?

This hibiscus corsage has five petals, two leaves, and a black center, which are all made following the basic axis method of beading on wire.

Wired Hibiscus Corsage

Designed by Mary Jo Hiney
Photograph on page 71.

Here's How:
1. For flower petal, cut one 40" length of wire.

2. Knot one end of wire.

3. To create basic axis, slip six mixed pink and rose beads on wire, positioning them 5" from knot. Extend wire 3" below last bead and fold wire back upon itself. Tightly wrap wire around itself just below last bead, leaving it extending to left of last bead. Using needle-nosed pliers, pull wire taut.

4. Smooth wire, bending it slightly from where wire extends at base of axis. Slip eight beads on wire and position it to lie snugly next to left side of axis.

5. Take wire across front of axis wire just above first bead on axis and tightly wrap it around axis wire, leaving wire extending to right of axis.

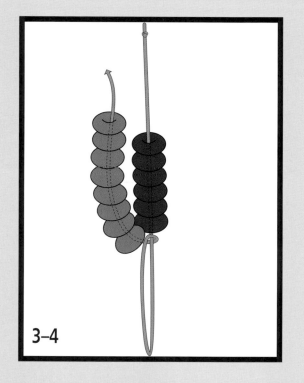

3–4

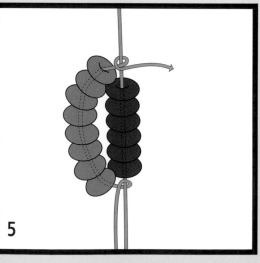

5

6. Slip twelve mixed pink and rose beads on wire and position it to lie snugly next to right side of axis.

7. Take wire across front of doubled axis wire just below last bead on left row 1 and tightly wrap it around axis wire leaving wire extending to left of axis.

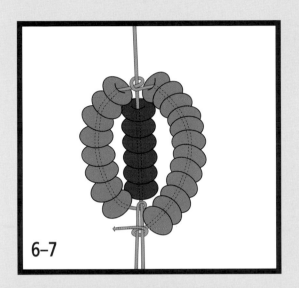

8. Repeat Steps 4–7 adding number of mixed pink and rose beads indicated for subsequent rows until there are six rows on each side of axis. Note: Make certain to keep axis straight—straighten axis after each additional row of beads is added.

Left, row 2: fifteen
Right, row 2: sixteen
Left, row 3: twenty
Right, row 3: twenty-two
Left, row 4: twenty-eight
Right, row 4: thirty-one
Left, row 5: thirty-four
Right, row 5: thirty-five
Left, row 6: forty
Right, row 6: forty-one

9. Tightly wrap wire from row 6 twice around doubled axis wire. Cut doubled wire at loop and twist all three wires together. Trim wire ends.

10. Cut knot from end of axis wire. Insert end of wire from back to front between right rows 5 and 6. Using needle-nosed pliers, wrap wire to back and pull taut. Cut wire close to rows.

11. Repeat Steps 1–10 for five petals.

12. Determine front and back side of each petal—wire wrappings are more prominent on back side. Position petals side to side in a circle to form flower and twist wires together.

13. For stamen, cut one 20" length of wire.

14. Knot one end of wire. Slip thirty medium green beads on wire, positioning them 3" from knot. Bend wire so beads form a loop. Wrap wire snugly around knotted end just below first and last bead, extending wire even with first loop. Using needle-nosed pliers, pull wire taut.

15. Slip thirty more medium green beads on wire. Bend wire to form second loop. Wrap wire snugly around itself at base of second loop and then around base of first loop, extending wire even with base of second loop. Continue in this manner to form eight loops, wrapping wire to previous loop each time.

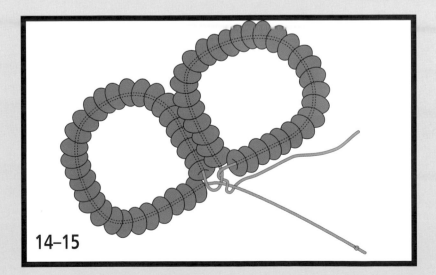

16. Wire first and last loop together.

17. Position stamen over center of petals. Twist all wires together.

18. For flower center, cut one 20" length of wire.

19. Repeat Steps 2–9, beginning with five black beads on axis wire and adding number of black beads indicated for subsequent rows until there are four rows on each side of axis.

Left, row 1: eight
Right, row 1: eleven
Left, row 2: twelve
Right, row 2: seventeen
Left, row 3: eighteen
Right, row 3: twenty-two

20. Cut knot from axis wire. Pull wire and twisted wires together as for strings on a bonnet, shaping beads so back side of flower center is within curve.

21. Position flower center over center of stamen and petals. Twist all wires together.

22. For leaf, cut one 36" length of wire.

23. Repeat Steps 2–10, beginning with sixteen light green beads on axis wire and adding number of light green beads indicated for subsequent rows until there are four rows on each side of axis.

Left, row 1: twenty
Right, row 1: twenty-two
Left, row 2: twenty-seven
Right, row 2: twenty-nine
Left, row 3: thirty-five
Right, row 3: thirty-six
Left, row 4: thirty-eight
Right, row 4: thirty-nine
Left, row 5: forty-four
Right, row 5: forty-four

24. Repeat Steps 22–23 for two leaves.

25. Determine front and back side of each leaf. Position leaves side to side and twist wires together. Beginning just below beads, wrap 1" of wires with florist tape.

26. Paint outer edge of each velvet leaf with burgundy paint. Allow to dry.

27. Moisten fingers. Working along one long edge of fabric, roll fabric so cut edge is hidden and becomes rolled.

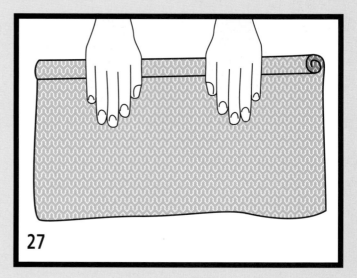

27

28. Using needle and thread, gather-stitch opposite long edge. Pull threads tightly, ruffling fabric. Position ruffle so it is snug against underside of flower. Knot thread.

29. Beginning just below underside of ruffle, wrap 1½" of flower wires with florist tape, forming a stem. Wrap wires of beaded leaves and velvet leaves onto stem.

30. Open pin back. Place metal back against stem, close to underside of flower. Wrap stem and pin back with florist tape. Continue wrapping stem to end of wires.

How do I string beads to create lace?

What You Need to Get Started:

<u>Beads:</u>
11/0 seed beads: matte green; matte purple

<u>Etc.:</u>
Beading needle
Fabric scissors
Iron and ironing board
Linen: sage green (⅛ yard); lavender (⅛ yard)
#2 pencil
Ruler
Sewing machine
Thread: sage green; lavender

"Lace" can be made with beads in a manner that is similar to the way lace is crocheted. Evenly spaced patterns of beads are worked in rounds or rows until a lacy look results.

Beaded Lace-edged Coasters
Photograph on page 75.

Here's How:
1. Cut two 5"-square pieces from each color of linen.

2. Place lavender fabric squares with right sides together. Sew all around edges with ½" seam allowance, leav-ing 2" open for turning. Trim seams, clip at corners, and turn right side out. Press edges flat and stitch opening closed to create coaster. Repeat for sage green fabric squares.

3. Mark back of each coaster in ½" intervals for working lace. Mark lavender coaster further by dividing each half inch into thirds.

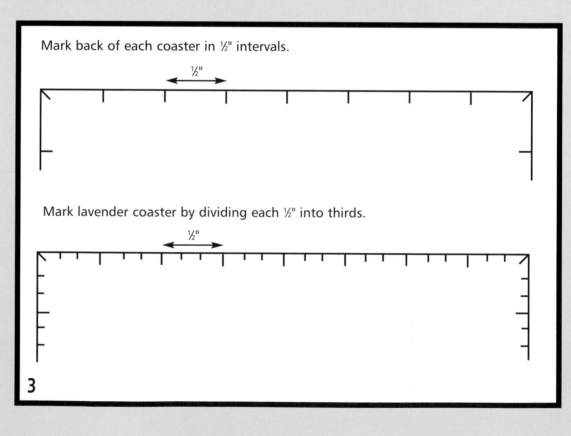

Mark back of each coaster in ½" intervals.

½"

Mark lavender coaster by dividing each ½" into thirds.

½"

3

4. Cut one 30" length of sage green thread and thread needle. For first round of beads on green coaster marked in ½" intervals, bring needle out at center mark on one side. Slip eleven beads on needle.

5. Insert needle into fabric at next mark, catching just enough fabric to be secure, and bring needle back through last bead on resulting loop.

6. Slip ten beads on needle.

7. Repeat Steps 5–6 at each interval all around coaster.

8. For second round on green coaster, bring needle out in fourth bead of first loop. Slip seven beads on needle.

9. Skip three beads on loop and run needle through eighth bead. Bring needle back through last bead on second round.

10. Slip six beads on needle and run needle through fourth bead on next loop. Bring needle back through last bead on second round.

11. Repeat Steps 9–10 from loop to loop all around coaster. Note: When looping around each corner, slip two additional beads on needle.

12. When beading is complete, run thread through beads into fabric and bury it in weave of fabric.

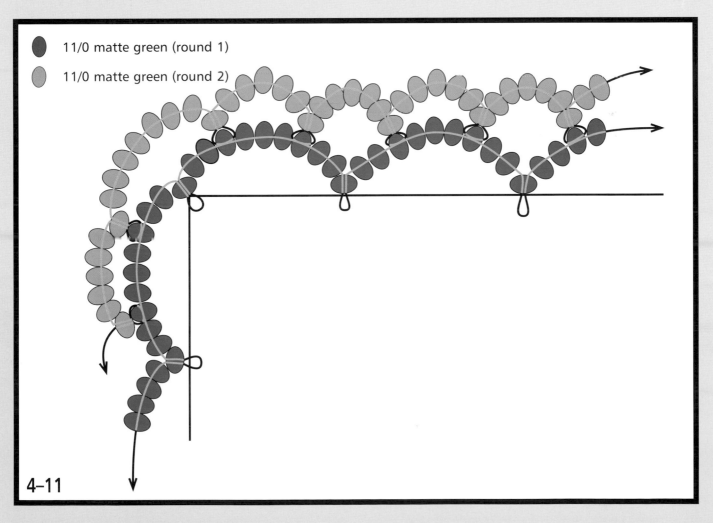

● 11/0 matte green (round 1)
● 11/0 matte green (round 2)

4-11

13. Cut one 30" length of lavender thread and thread needle. For first round of beads on lavender coaster, bring needle out at any mark on one side. Slip eight beads on needle.

14. Insert needle into fabric at next mark, catching just enough fabric to be secure, and bring needle back through last three beads on resulting loop.

15. Slip five beads on needle.

16. Repeat Steps 14–15 at each interval all around coaster. Note: When looping around each corner, slip two additional beads on needle, insert needle into fabric at corner, catching just enough fabric to be secure, and bring needle back through last four beads on resulting loop. Slip six beads on needle and work loop from corner to next side.

17. When first round is complete, secure thread and trim it close.

18. For second round on lavender coaster, thread needle. Bring needle out at one corner through six beads as indicated.

19. Slip six beads on needle.

20. Run needle through third bead again, looping last three beads on thread. Guide beads toward existing beadwork, taking up slack in thread and forming a "picot" or three-bead group.

21. Slip two beads on needle and run needle through indicated beads on next two loops.

22. Repeat Steps 19–21 from loop to loop all around coaster. Note: When looping around each corner, run needle through indicated beads to form a separate picot.

23. When beading is complete, run thread through beads into fabric and bury it in weave of fabric.

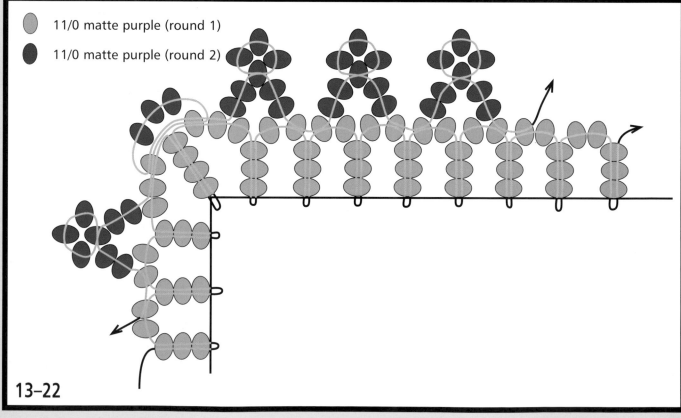

11/0 matte purple (round 1)

11/0 matte purple (round 2)

13–22

Design Tips:

The best choice for beading lace is 11/0 seed beads, largely because they have rounded edges which allow flexibility in the way the beads lie against each other.

Troubleshooting:

For additional threadings, refer to Adding a New Length of Thread on page 19.

4
project

What You Need to Get Started:

Beads:
10 mm firepolish crystals: bronze (7)
4 mm round beads: matte gold (14)
11/0 seed beads: black (12); dark bronze (150); metallic gold (150); pewter (350)

Etc.:
Barrel clasp: gold-finished
Card stock
Craft scissors
Double-sided fusible webbing
Ear findings: matte gold-finished, celtic-type pattern (2)
#9 embroidery needle
Head pins: gold-finished, .22-diameter, 1¼"-long (2)
Lightweight leather for backing: black, 3" square
Round-nosed pliers
Wire cutters

How do I combine stringing with surface beading?

This project demonstrates how surface beading on card stock can become an attractive pendant by adding on fringes for embellishment and strings of beads for a necklace. Simple component techniques are used for the matching earrings.

Celtic Knot Necklace & Earrings
Photograph on page 78.

Here's How:
1. Photocopy Celtic Knot Pattern directly onto card stock.

2. Trim the card stock to ½" all around pattern edge, keeping corners somewhat rounded to avoid catching thread.

3. Cut one 30" length of thread and thread needle.

4. Refer to Steps 8–9 for Technique 10 on pages 41–42. For curves and outlines, sew metallic gold and pewter 11/0 seed beads onto card stock. Run backtracking thread through beads.

5. Refer to Step 7 and Step 10 for Technique 10. Fill in background areas with black and dark bronze 11/0 seed beads.

6. For one drop on pendant, bring needle to front surface at one dot. Slip beads of each drop on needle. Skipping last seed bead, run thread back through all beads. Repeat for each drop.

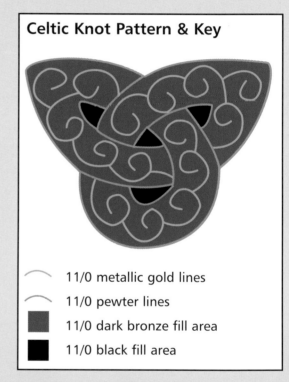

Celtic Knot Pattern & Key

⌒ 11/0 metallic gold lines
⌒ 11/0 pewter lines
■ 11/0 dark bronze fill area
■ 11/0 black fill area

7. For one necklace strand on pendant, bring needle out at either dot on top left edge. Slip four pewter seed beads, one matte gold round bead, one fire-polish crystal, one matte gold round bead, and one dark bronze seed bead on needle. Slip pewter seed beads on needle to 7½" length.

8. Sew one part of clasp onto bead strand, looping thread back through

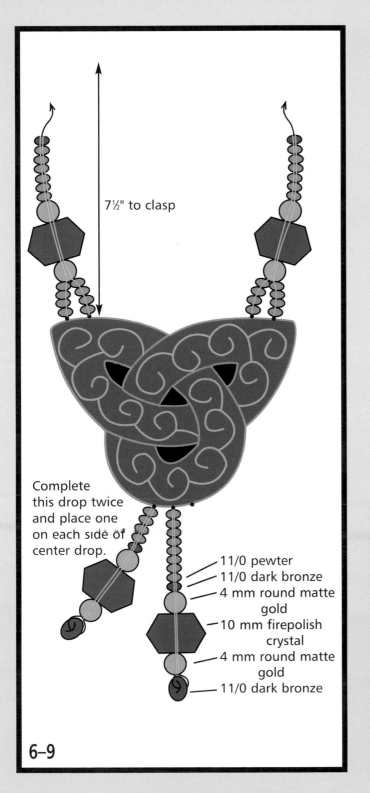

7½" to clasp

Complete this drop twice and place one on each side of center drop.

11/0 pewter
11/0 dark bronze
4 mm round matte gold
10 mm firepolish crystal
4 mm round matte gold
11/0 dark bronze

6–9

last few beads until clasp is secure. Run thread back through all—except last four seed beads—on strand.

9. Add four more pewter 11/0 seed beads and take needle through remaining dot.

10. Bury thread in back of stitching and trim excess close to project.

11. Repeat Steps 6–9 for necklace strand on top right edge of pendant.

12. Refer to Steps 10–12 for Technique 10. To finish back of surface-beaded project, apply fusible webbing and leather.

13. To make earrings, slip beads for each drop on head pin. Using wire cutters, trim head pin to ⅜". Using round-nosed pliers, form an open loop. Slip loop of head pin on ear finding and carefully close loop.

Troubleshooting:

For additional threadings, refer to Adding a New Length of Thread on page 19.

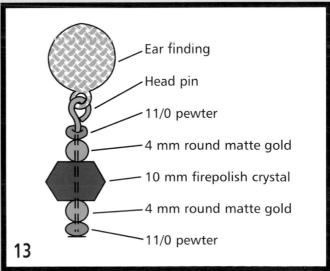

Ear finding
Head pin
11/0 pewter
4 mm round matte gold
10 mm firepolish crystal
4 mm round matte gold
11/0 pewter

13

How do I finish a beaded piece of needlepoint canvas?

This eyeglass case is worked in beaded needlepoint on #14 interlock needlepoint canvas with 11/0 seed beads. It is finished with coordinating fabric that adds to the elegant look of the beaded design.

Oriental Carpet Eyeglass Case
Photograph on page 81.

Here's How:
1. Refer to Steps 1–3 for Technique 12 on page 47. Following Oriental Carpet Pattern on page 80, work from top row to bottom row. Note: The last row charted is the center row in the design.

2. Turn chart 180° and continue working design from center row—but not repeating center row.

3. Using steam iron, steam back of work and reshape it so it is squared. Note: Take care when handling glass beads that have been under the iron as they can be quite hot to the touch.

4. Trim canvas to ½" around design and clip corners.

5. Using pressed and trimmed beadwork as a template, cut two pieces from lining fabric and one from backing fabric.

6. Press canvas edges under finished beadwork. Press edges of remaining three pieces under to same size.

7. Stitch one lining piece onto back of beadwork, hiding raw edges.

What You Need to Get Started:

Beads:
11/0 seed beads:
  aqua (1000);
  dark blue (900);
  pale blue (300);
  light green (100);
  pink (1100); light purple (308);
  medium purple (280); red (240);
  yellow (960)

Etc.:
#9 embroidery needle
Fabric for lining and backing (⅛ yard each)
Fabric scissors
#14 interlock needlepoint canvas: 5" x 9"
Steam iron and ironing board
Thread: off-white

Clip all corners before pressing edges under.

6

Stitch lining fabric onto back of beadwork.

7

79

8. Stitch remaining lining and backing pieces so raw edges are together.

9. When both backing and beadwork have been lined, stitch them together, leaving one edge open to form eyeglass case.

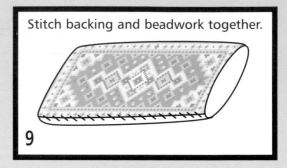

Stitch backing and beadwork together.

9

Troubleshooting:

For additional threadings, refer to Adding a New Length of Thread on page 19.

Oriental Carpet Pattern & Key

Center row —

▨ 11/0 yellow	▨ 11/0 light purple	▨ 11/0 dark blue
▨ 11/0 pink	▪ 11/0 medium purple	▨ 11/0 aqua
▪ 11/0 red	▫ 11/0 pale blue	▨ 11/0 light green

6 project

What You Need to Get Started:

Beads:
11/0 seed beads: matte aqua (5 grams); black (5 grams); metallic gold (200); lime (60); lavender (75); light orange (30); purple (20); rose (50)

Etc.:
Clasp: gold-finished
Embroidery scissors
Jewelry glue
Leather cord: medium weight, 18"-long
Needle-nosed pliers
Pressure crimps: gold-finished (2)
6 mm rings: gold-finished (2)
Sewing needle
Thread: tan

How do I join squared needle-weaving?

This design is worked in needle-weaving. The leather strap is sewn onto the finished piece; pressure crimps and clasp are added to the ends of the leather.

Woven Bag Necklace
Photograph on page 84.

Here's How:

1. Refer to Steps 1–14 for Technique 15 on pages 53–55. Following Woven Bag Necklace Pattern on opposite page, weave entire piece. Work the flap as charted, adding and decreasing beads in length as indicated. Note: The pattern is not shown in its entirety; the body of the bag is made of alternating vertical rows of black and matte aqua, each eighty-one beads long.

2. When entire piece has been woven, fold body of bag in half, allowing three horizontal rows between top edge of body and beginning of flap for attaching leather cord.

3. Join sides of body by repeating Steps 4–7 for Technique 15, treating doubled first and last rows as if each were now both Row 1 and Row 2.

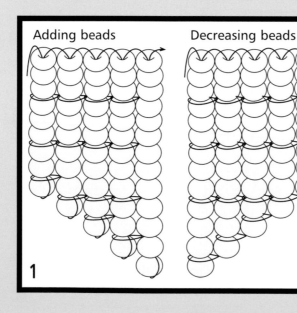

Adding beads   Decreasing beads

1

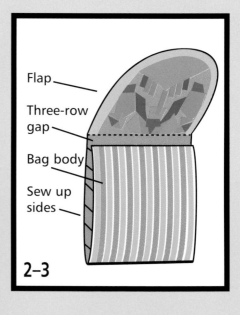

Flap

Three-row gap

Bag body

Sew up sides

2–3

Woven Bag Necklace Pattern & Key

Body of bag, each row 81 beads

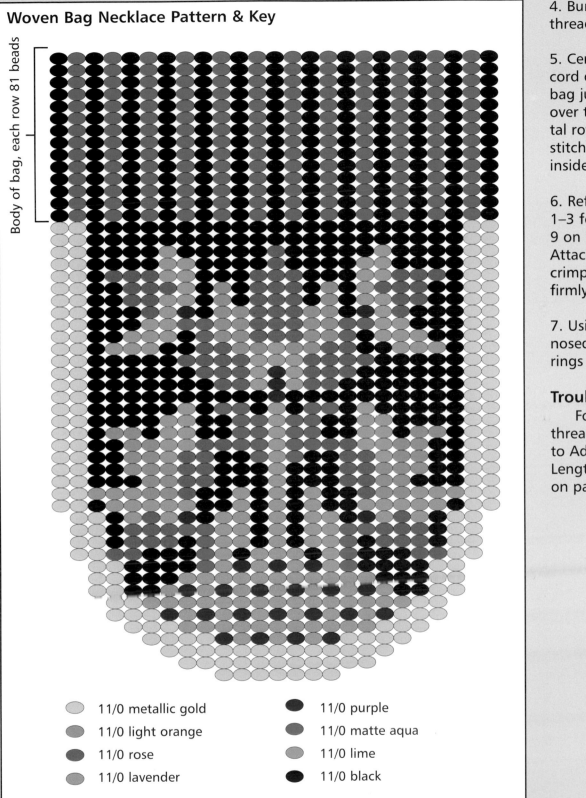

○ 11/0 metallic gold	● 11/0 purple
○ 11/0 light orange	● 11/0 matte aqua
● 11/0 rose	○ 11/0 lime
○ 11/0 lavender	● 11/0 black

4. Bury excess thread in weave.

5. Center leather cord on inside of bag just below flap over three horizontal rows. Whipstitch cord onto inside of bag.

6. Refer to Steps 1–3 for Technique 9 on page 38. Attach pressure crimps, securing firmly with glue.

7. Using needle-nosed pliers, attach rings and clasp.

Troubleshooting:
For additional threadings, refer to Adding a New Length of Thread on page 19.

How do I shape needle-weaving and add fringes?

What You Need to Get Started:

This squared needle-weaving design is made up of delica beads. Because of their uniformity of shape and size, delica beads create a beautiful effect when woven. The fringes and necklace strands are made up of thoughtfully placed colors combined with ornamental 6/0 seed beads and faceted crystals.

<u>Beads</u>:
Delica beads:
   metallic gold (462); light green (169); dark green (89); ivory (289); dark blue-lavender (1577); light blue-lavender (277); light rose (146); dark rose (80)
6 mm faceted crystals: light blue (27)
6/0 seed beads: lavender (37)

<u>Etc.</u>:
Barrel clasp: gold-finished
#9 embroidery needle
Embroidery scissors
Thread: tan

Squared Floral Necklace
Photograph on page 88.

Here's How:
1. Following Squared Floral Necklace Pattern on page 87, string beads for Row 1 from top to bottom. Skipping last bead, insert needle back through all beads. Note: The needle should emerge from the top bead of Row 1.

2. String beads for Row 2, from top to bottom. Add first fringe by continuing to string as charted from top to bottom. Skipping last bead, insert needle back through all beads on fringe. Insert needle into loop exposed at bottom of Row 1. Pull thread gently until entire second row is taut, but not tight, and beads rest against first row without puckering. Note: When forming fringes, the tension of the thread is important. Try to leave enough slack so that the fringes move freely, but not so much that there is a lot of visible thread. Part of the beauty of fringes is their motion. Lack of motion impedes the beauty of the overall design.

3. Insert needle into last three beads of Row 2, and bring thread out until it is taut, but not tight. Loop thread around Row 1 so it is nestled between corresponding beads of Row 1. Insert needle into next three beads of Row 2, bringing needle out again between subsequent beads on Row 2. Again, thread should be taut, but not tight.

4. Loop thread around Row 1 so it is nestled between corresponding beads of Row 1. Insert needle into next three beads on Row 2 and continue this looping and inserting process until thread emerges from bead 1 of Row 2.

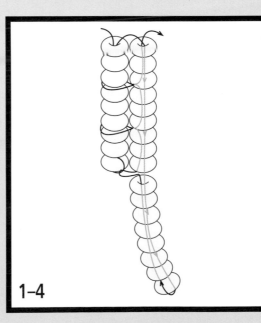

1–4

5. Repeat Steps 1–4 for all subsequent rows of pattern and fringes.

6. Cut one 24" length of thread and thread needle.

7. Attach thread at outermost top row of either side of foundation pattern by running it through several of beads in foundation until secure or by tying it onto end of thread left from weaving.

8. Slip beads on needle as indicated. Slip dark blue-lavender delica beads on needle to 8½" length. Note: There are two patterns of strands, "dots" and "Xs", which emanate from the top of rows marked on the foundation pattern.

9. Take needle through loop of one end of barrel clasp and then reinsert it into top bead of necklace strand. Run thread through all beads on strand until reaching foundation pattern.

10. Run thread through beads in foundation pattern and bring out at next marker.

11. Repeat Steps 8–10 until all strings are attached.

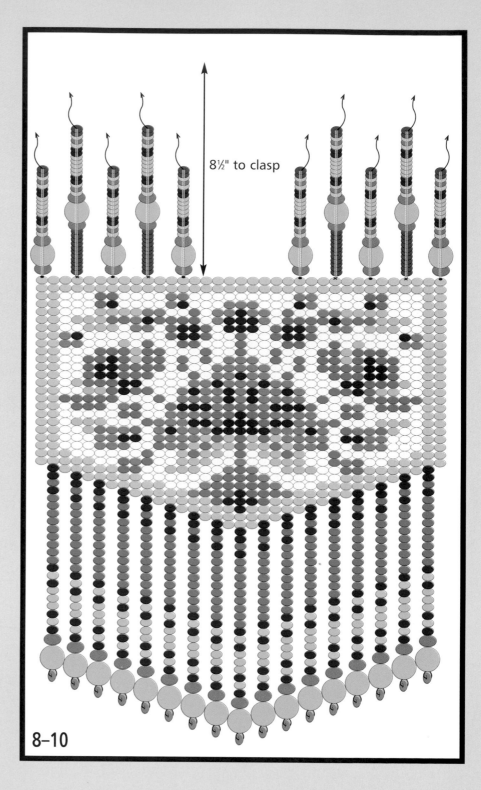

8½" to clasp

8–10

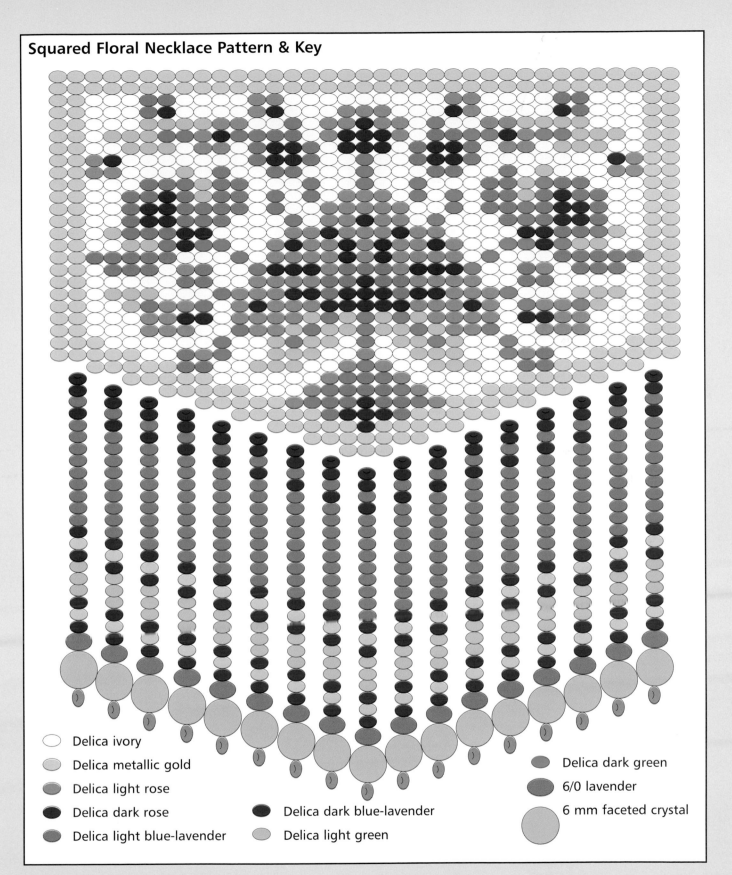

Squared Floral Necklace Pattern & Key

○ Delica ivory
○ Delica metallic gold
○ Delica light rose
● Delica dark rose
● Delica light blue-lavender
● Delica dark blue-lavender
○ Delica light green
● Delica dark green
● 6/0 lavender
○ 6 mm faceted crystal

How do I create a tube with needle-weaving?

This interesting necklace uses squared needle-weaving and demonstrates how to join the weave to form a tube. It is then embellished with a turquoise drop attached to a band of bugle beads formed by double needle-weaving.

Beads:
#3 bugle beads:
  gold (18)
11/0 seed beads:
  dark aqua (250);
  light aqua (480);
  metallic copper
  (250); cream
  (1800); metallic
  gold (350)

Etc.:
Barrel clasp: gold-
  finished
Clothesline:
  ¼"-diameter,
  18"-long
Craft scissors
Sewing needles (2)
Thread: tan
Turquoise carved
  drop

Woven Southwest Tube Necklace
Photograph on page 91.

Here's How:
Note: An arrowhead-shaped drop was used to embellish this piece, but any shaped drop will work.

1. Refer to Steps 1–14 for Technique 15 on pages 53–55. Following Woven Southwest Tube Necklace Pattern on page 90, weave right half of piece, beginning at center row as indicated on pattern. Weave vertical rows as charted, repeating final section until length of half-strip is 8½" long.

2. Attach thread at center row (first woven row), rotate work piece 180° and repeat pattern until both ends are identical. Note: As there is no front or back to the design, rotate or flip the work piece and complete the weave in a manner that is most comfortable for you.

3. Wrap width of woven piece around clothesline, matching top and bottom beads of each vertical row.

4. Attach new thread at one end of weave. Take needle through last three beads on first row and continue through first three beads on same row. Take thread through first three beads on next row and continue through last three beads of same row. Continue weaving back and forth until entire length has been joined together.

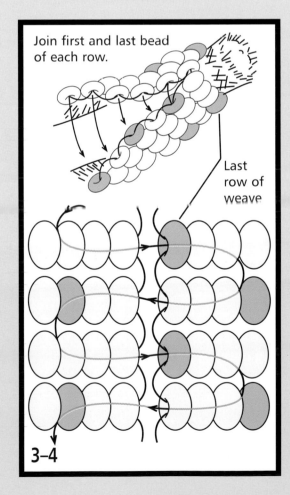

Join first and last bead of each row.

Last row of weave

3–4

5. Trim each end of clothesline very close to end of weave.

6. Attach new thread at one end of weave. Take needle through three beads on last row of weave. Slip two cream 11/0 seed beads on needle and run needle back through first three and next three seed beads on woven row. Slip two more beads on needle and continue in this manner all around until twelve beads have been added onto weave.

7. Take needle through first two beads on row of twelve. Slip one cream 11/0 seed bead on needle and run needle back through first two and next two seed beads on row. Slip one more bead on needle and continue in this manner all around until six beads have been added on. Run thread through last six beads and pull thread taut so gap closes.

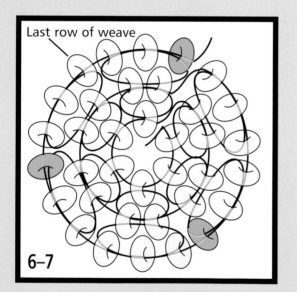

Last row of weave

6–7

8. Repeat Steps 6–7 for remaining end.

9. Sew one part of clasp onto each finished end, looping thread back through last few beads until clasp is secure. Bury thread in weave.

90

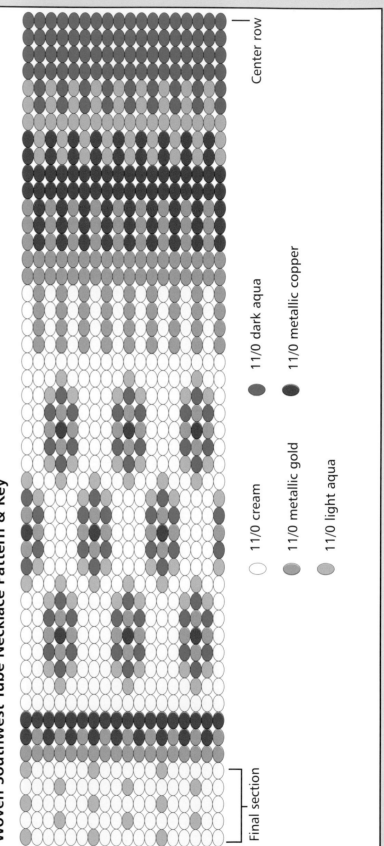

Woven Southwest Tube Necklace Pattern & Key

Center row

11/0 dark aqua

11/0 metallic copper

11/0 cream

11/0 metallic gold

11/0 light aqua

Final section

10. Refer to Steps 1–5 for Technique 13 on page 50, substituting two needles and thread for wire. Weave eighteen bugle beads together in a strip. Join length together in a circle around center of tube necklace.

11. Sew turquoise drop onto one bugle bead in ring and bury excess thread in weave.

9
project

What You Need to Get Started:

Beads:
6 mm aventurine flat beads with hole through length (5)
Delica beads:
  cream (400); galvanized gold (50); galvanized light green (80); galvanized dark pink (75); galvanized light pink (160)

Etc.:
Ear wires: gold-finished (2)
#9 embroidery needles (2)
Embroidery scissors
Pin back: 1½"
Needle-nosed pliers
4 mm rings: gold-finished (2)
Thread: off-white

How do I embellish brick stitch needle-weaving?

This set is worked in brick stitch, which is ideally suited to use in small jewelry items because the weave is strong and inflexible, so items hold their intended shape. This rigidity also makes it possible to attach heavier beads at the points of the design for attractive dangles.

Brick Stitch Pin & Earrings
Photograph on page 94.

Here's How:
Note: This design uses the top row of the pin as the foundation row.

1. Refer to Steps 1–6 for Technique 16 on pages 56–57. Following Brick Stitch Pin Pattern on opposite page, form foundation (top) row. Note: The thread that would ordinarily be used to work upward will be used to sew the finished beadwork to the pin back, so do not cut it.

2. Work consecutive rows until completing row 17. Weave thread through first and second bead on row 17 and bring needle out at bottom of third bead on row to begin row 18. Continue working remaining rows until pattern is complete.

3. Using thread end at bottom of pattern, slip one galvanized dark pink delica bead, one aventurine bead, and one galvanized dark pink delica bead on needle. Run needle back through aventurine and first galvanized dark pink delica bead.

4. Take needle up through cream delica beads on right side of woven piece. Bring needle out at bottom of second to last bead on row 17.

5. Repeat Step 3 at base of row 17.

6. Take needle up through last cream delica bead on row 17. Working from right to left, weave thread in and out of each bead on row 17 until reaching second bead on row.

7. Bring needle out at bottom of bead and repeat Step 3. Bury excess thread in weave.

8. Using thread at top of pattern, whipstitch pin back onto back top edge of woven piece.

(continued on page 94)

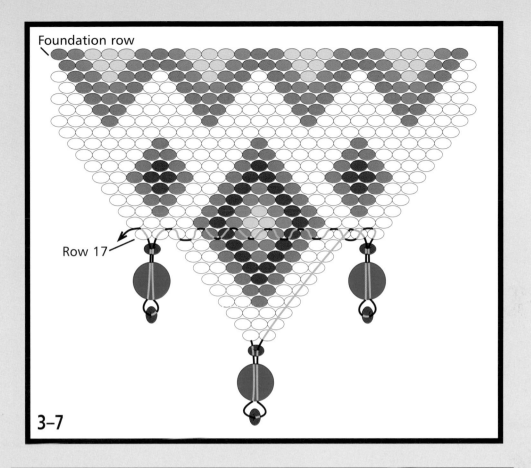

Foundation row

Row 17

3–7

Brick Stitch Pin Pattern & Key

Foundation row

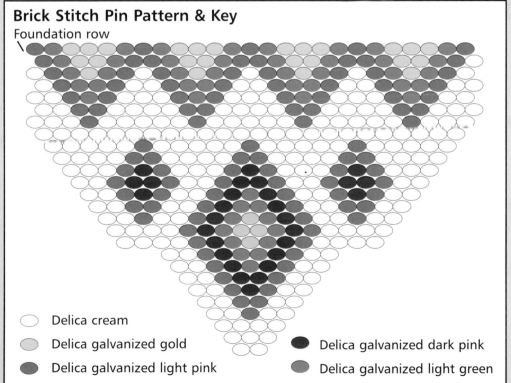

○ Delica cream

○ Delica galvanized gold

● Delica galvanized light pink

● Delica galvanized dark pink

● Delica galvanized light green

(continued from page 92)

9. For earrings, refer to Steps 1–7 for Technique 16. Following Brick Stitch Earring Pattern, form foundation row. Work consecutive rows to complete one full pattern. Repeat for second full pattern.

10. Repeat Step 3 for each. Bury excess thread in weave.

11. Using thread end at top of each pattern, take needle through top two beads and sew on one 4 mm ring. Bury excess thread in weave.

12. Using needle-nosed pliers, open loop on each ear wire. Slip ring on and close loop.

Foundation row

9–10

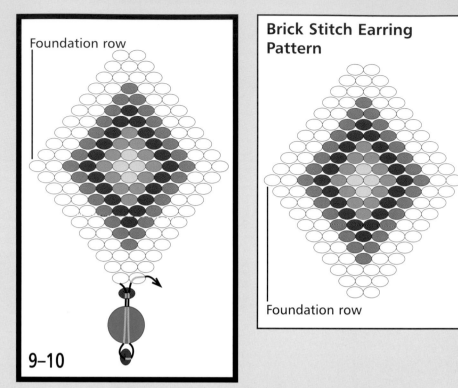

Brick Stitch Earring Pattern

Foundation row

How do I increase and decrease rows using peyote stitch needle-weaving?

This design is woven flat and then shaped to form a packet-type case. A felt pad is sewn into the center to hold your needles in place. In working this piece, you will not only solidify your basic peyote stitch technique, but you will also learn to increase and decrease at the row's end.

What You Need to Get Started:

Beads:
11/0 seed beads: silver-lined denim blue (260); dark metallic copper (800); gold (520); light green (54); pink (52); red (16)

Etc.:
Beading needle
Fabric scissors
Felt: gold, 2" square
Grosgrain ribbon, ¼"-wide: gold, 12"-long
Pinking shears
Thread: taupe

Peyote Stitch Needlecase
Photograph on page 97.

Here's How:
1. Refer to Steps 1–7 for Technique 17 on pages 58–59. Following Peyote Stitch Needlecase Pattern on page 96, leave 5"–6" thread, begin at top peak, and slip beads for first two rows on needle. Note: The long thread will be used later to sew on one tying ribbon. If the long thread is in the way, tape it to a surface until several rows of the weave have been established. This will also provide some stability during the first few rows.

of an increase row, so when you work the next row into a previous increase, make certain that beads lie flat so thread runs through the proper bead.

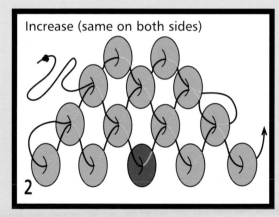

Increase (same on both sides)

2. For top half of design, continue working each individual bead between two beads of previous row, increasing at sides as indicated. Note: The beads and thread may have a tendency to twist out of position at the beginning

First two rows

3. For bottom half of design, continue working each individual bead between two beads of previous row, decreasing at sides as indicated.

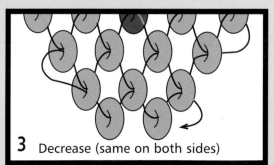

Decrease (same on both sides)

4. When weave is complete, leave 5"–6" thread at end. Note: This thread will be used to sew on the other tying ribbon.

5. Shape needle case by folding side flaps in on body of case.

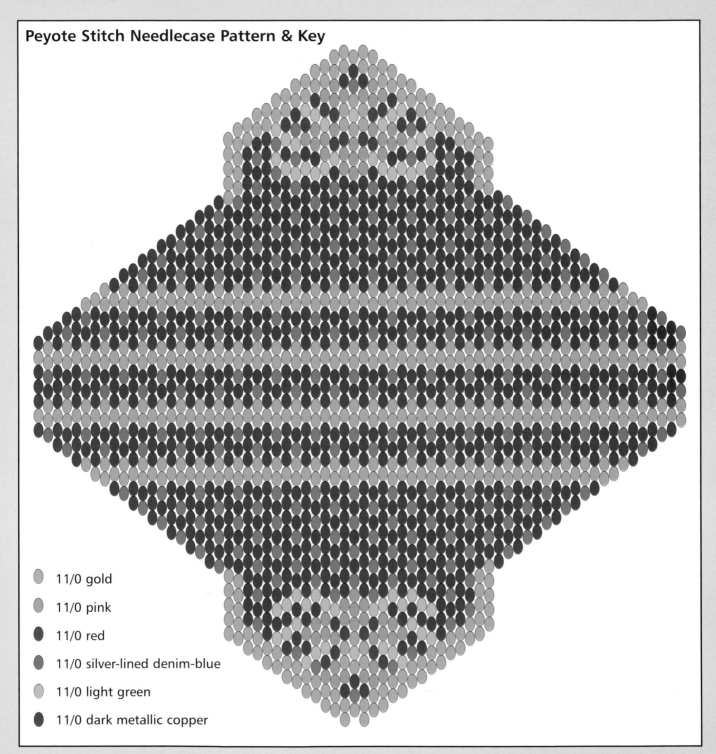

Peyote Stitch Needlecase Pattern & Key

- 11/0 gold
- 11/0 pink
- 11/0 red
- 11/0 silver-lined denim-blue
- 11/0 light green
- 11/0 dark metallic copper

6. Using pinking shears, trim felt piece to ¼" smaller all around than center of case. Center and tack felt onto beadwork.

7. Using fabric scissors, cut ribbon in half. Using long thread ends left in weaving, sew each piece onto point of top and bottom flaps. Bury excess thread in weave.

11
project

What You Need to Get Started:

Beads:
11/0 seed beads:
  dark blue (2
  hanks); dark
  medium blue (2
  hanks); medium
  blue (3 hanks);
  pale blue (1
  hank); white
  (6 hanks)
6/0 seed beads:
  medium blue
  (72)
6 mm x 10 mm
  teardrop crystals:
  light blue (36)

Etc.:
Beading loom to
  accommodate 36
  warp threads,
  each 20" long
Beading needles:
  long with very
  small eyes
#10 between
  needle
#9 embroidery
  needle
Jewelry glue
Lamp shade: 4"-
  diameter top,
  clamp-on style
  with paper
  removed
Thread: white
  (1 spool)

How do I join loomed panels and attach them to a frame?

This design is created by joining six loomed panels of beads together and then sewing the assembled piece onto a 4" lamp shade frame. You will weave three each of two different panel designs and alternate them in the final piece.

Loomed Mandarin Lamp Shade
Photograph on page 101.

Here's How:
1. Following manufacturer's instructions, warp loom with thirty-six warp threads. Note: Roll the warp on one end if necessary, but make certain that the entire length of the warp is at least 20".

2. Refer to Steps 2–5 for Technique 18 on page 61. Allowing 4" of unloomed warp and following Mandarin Lamp Shade Pattern #1 on opposite page, work weft threads until reaching point where rows begin to decrease in size. Note: Roll the loomed beadwork onto the starting end of the loom if necessary to keep working.

3. To decrease number of beads on rows, slip beads on needle and pass under warp threads, positioning beads and threads so each bead falls between two warp threads as charted and ignoring outer warp threads. After beads are seated into warp, pass needle back through beads so weft thread goes over warp threads. Note: As work continues, multiple warp threads will be ignored. All warp threads will eventually be worked into the finishing.

4. Remove panel from loom, leaving as much warp thread as possible.

5. Repeat Steps 1–4 for two more panels.

6. Following Mandarin Lamp Shade Pattern #2 on opposite page, repeat Steps 1–4 for three panels.

7. At top end of each panel, tie four consecutive warp threads together, positioning knot very close to weave.

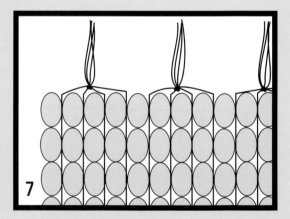

8. Apply dot of glue onto each knot and trim tied warp ends to less than 1". Note: These ends and knots will eventually be hidden behind the beads when the top edge is sewn onto the shade frame.

(continued on page 100)

Mandarin Lamp Shade Pattern #1

Mandarin Lamp Shade Pattern #2

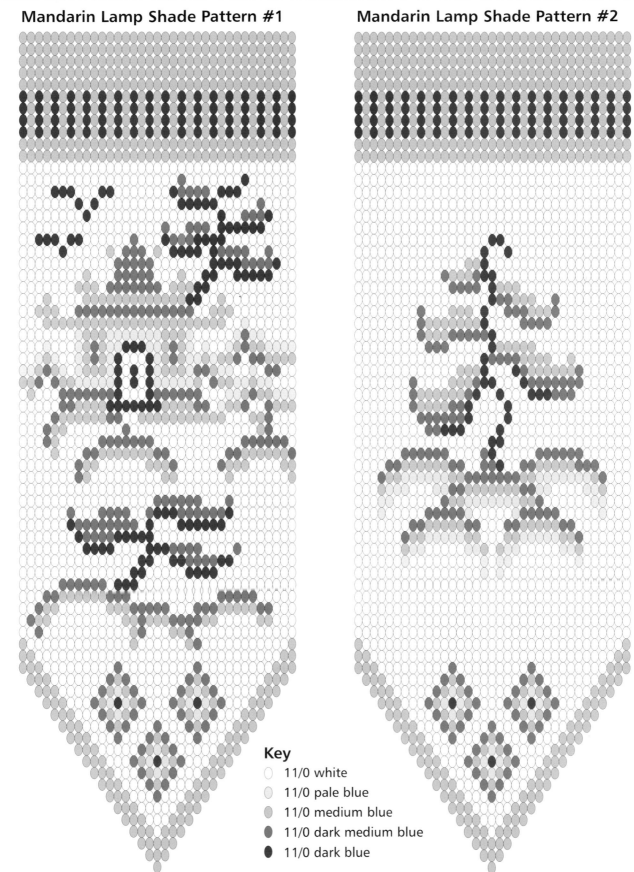

Key

- ○ 11/0 white
- ○ 11/0 pale blue
- ● 11/0 medium blue
- ● 11/0 dark medium blue
- ● 11/0 dark blue

99

(continued from page 98)

9. Refer to Step 4 of Project 8 on page 89. Join all six panels together—two at a time and alternating panels—taking needle through last three beads on first row of one panel and continuing through first three beads on same row of remaining panel. Weave thread back and forth until entire length has been joined together.

10. Bury any excess joining thread in weave.

11. To finish bottom edge of shade, separate consecutive warp threads into groups of six threads, beginning with three threads from each side of each panel point.

12. Beginning at panel point, trim all six threads as one for clean edge. Thread #9 embroidery needle with these threads. Slip one 6/0 bead, one crystal, and one 6/0 bead on needle. Knot threads, positioning beads very close to woven panel. Note: It may be necessary to knot over the first knot one or more times to make certain that the beads are secure.

13. Apply small dot of glue just beyond knot and take needle back through beads until only knot remains visible beyond beads. Trim excess thread that was pulled through beads close to first 6/0 bead, taking care to avoid cutting any threads that secure beads.

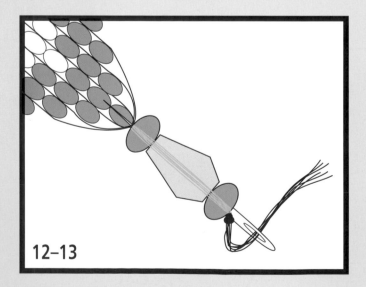

12–13

14. Repeat Steps 12–13 for each panel point.

15. Repeat Steps 12–13 for each group of six warp threads (three warp threads from each side) joining seams.

16. Repeat Steps 12–13 for each remaining group of six warp threads.

17. After all drops are in place, pin top edge of assembled piece onto shade frame and baste-stitch in place. Note: As this is a circular design, it makes no difference where the assembled panel is positioned on the frame.

18. Using #10 between needle and thread, sew panel onto frame by wrapping top three to four rows of beading around frame, tucking knots along top edge into sewing, and securing edge with in-and-out stitches through weave. Note: Each stitch that shows on the outside of the design should be no wider than one bead so it will not be noticeable.

19. Carefully trim excess threads.

Design Tips:

Use your finger to press the beads up through the warp to make it easier to run the needle through the beads on the return trip.

Make certain to choose a lamp base that is a solid neutral color. It should accent the woven piece, not detract from it.

Try a different color scheme for working this design. Substitute shades of red or brown or yellow to accent the decor of your own home.

Substitute a different design for the one that is charted. Look through cross-stitch and needle-point books to find a pleasing design. Make certain the horizontal and vertical counts are the same as the original. Each charted square on the cross-stitch or needlepoint graph will represent one bead.

101

designed by Ann Benson

designed by Ann Benson

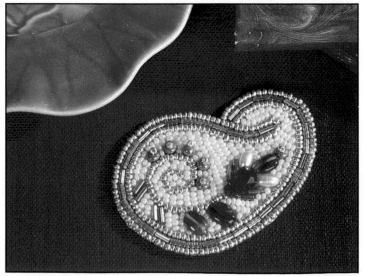

designed by Ann Benson

designed by Ann Benson

designed by Ann Benson

designed by Ann Benson

Section 4: *gallery of artists*

designed by Ann Benson

designed by Ann Benson

designed by Jackie Hirsh

Jackie Hirsh found her creative self four years ago after years as a high school French teacher and psychiatric social worker. Since that time, she has been making beadwork and says that it provides her with a loving connection to her late mother and grandmother, both of whom did beautiful handwork. It was actually during the early days of her beading obsession that got her in touch with memories when she was just six or seven years old of her mother beading handbags. She loved parading around with those bejeweled purses which are the inspiration for the handbags and evening purses she creates today.

designed by Jackie Hirsh

designed by Jackie Hirsh

designed by Jackie Hirsh

Christiana Lapatina Johnson is a California-based designer with extensive experience in hand beadwork, applique, and print design specializing in imports. She is one of the premiere hand beadwork importers in the world. Unique in her design approach, she has a special style that transforms beautiful glass beads into visual works of art.

She has found success in designing collections of beaded objects. All of her frames, lamps, pillows, and albums work together to complement any home. She caters to a fashion-forward clientele and has a beaded bag, belt, or baguette for any occasion.

Looking to the future, Christiana will introduce a signature line of hand-beaded and embroidered clothing items in sumptuous fabrics and rich leathers.

designed by Christiana Lapatina Johnson

designed by Christiana Lapatina Johnson

designed by Christiana Lapatina Johnson

designed by Christiana Lapatina Johnson

designed by Sharon Bateman

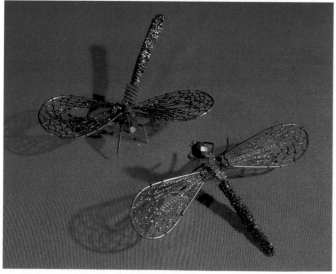

designed by Sharon Bateman

designed by Sharon Bateman

designed by Sharon Bateman

Sharon Bateman is a free-lance writer and designer, whose work has appeared many times in various books and magazines such as *Making Bead and Wire Jewelry*, *Bead & Button*, *Lapidary Journal*, and *Jewelry Crafts*. She is the inventor and manufacturer of Sharondipity Tube Looms, a series of looms geared for amulet bags and bracelets that eliminate the need to tie off warp threads.

Sharon's passion for beads covers a wide range of stitches and techniques—her favorite is the square stitch because of its versatility in doing dimensional work. She has several techniques that are unique to her work, including the Corkscrew Fringe, the Bead Wrap, and the Morning Rose. Her other interests include watercolors, pastels, airbrushing, and stone carving. Sharon resides in Northern Idaho with her husband and three boys.

designed by Sharon Bateman

Ginger Sizemore originally hails from Colorado, but now lives with her husband Sherman and their exotic parrots and macaws on a macadamia nut farm on the Big Island of Hawaii.

When she was a child, she was fascinated with two things—her mother's button box and her father's collection of seashells, accumulated during his navy days. These two elements sparked her interest in jewelry making, and as a child, Ginger would make necklaces and sell them on consignment in local shops.

When Ginger completed high school and business school, she had the opportunity to move to Hawaii, where she began her own seashell collection and continued to create jewelry and wearable art.

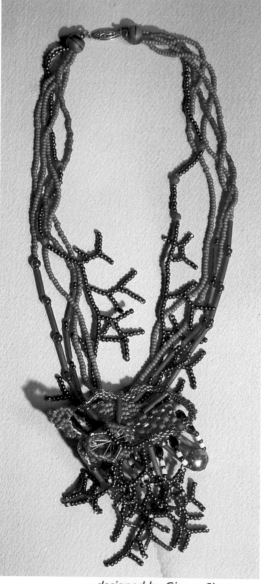

designed by Ginger Sizemore

designed by Ginger Sizemore

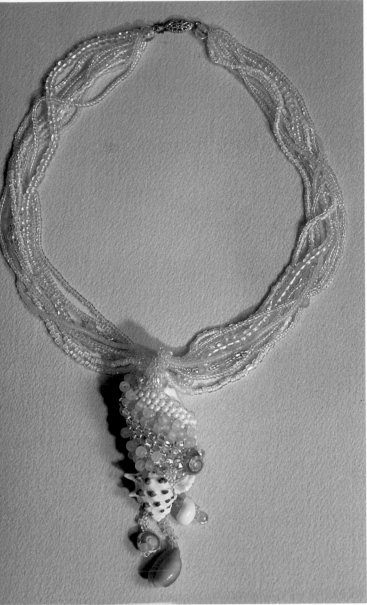

designed by Ginger Sizemore

Ginger fulfilled her dream of owning her own store in which to sell her creations. She retired from owning and managing eight unique shops after sixteen years.

Currently, Ginger teaches jewelry making and continues to create one-of-a-kind art, which she supplies to local boutiques.

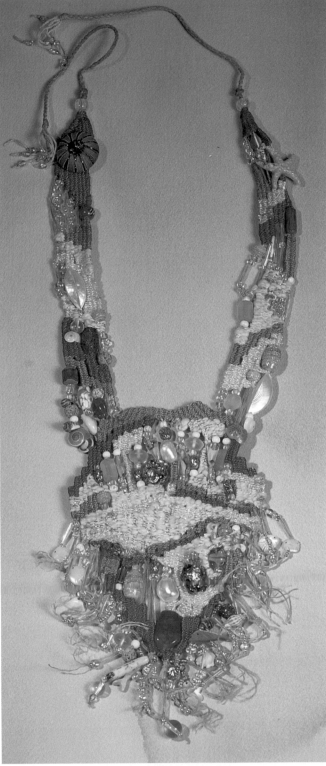

designed by Ginger Sizemore

Professionally, **Kathy Rice** works as a computer graphics artist. In her spare time, she enjoys doing beadwork. She started in 1989 after seeing a pair of Indian earrings she wanted. She felt she could not justify paying the $15 that seller was asking. So Kathy went to a bead store, bought a book and some beads, and spent $45 instead. Now many years and several thousands of dollars later, she realizes that they were practically giving those original Indian earrings away for the price of $15. She has become a bead addict and teacher.

designed by Kathy Rice

designed by Kathy Rice

designed by Kathy Rice

Metric equivalency chart

mm-millimetres cm-centimetres
inches to millimetres and centimetres

inches	mm	cm	inches	cm	inches	cm
⅛	3	0.3	9	22.9	30	76.2
¼	6	0.6	10	25.4	31	78.7
⅜	10	1.0	11	27.9	32	81.3
½	13	1.3	12	30.5	33	83.8
⅝	16	1.6	13	33.0	34	86.4
¾	19	1.9	14	35.6	35	88.9
⅞	22	2.2	15	38.1	36	91.4
1	25	2.5	16	40.6	37	94.0
1¼	32	3.2	17	43.2	38	96.5
1½	38	3.8	18	45.7	39	99.1
1¾	44	4.4	19	48.3	40	101.6
2	51	5.1	20	50.8	41	104.1
2½	64	6.4	21	53.3	42	106.7
3	76	7.6	22	55.9	43	109.2
3½	89	8.9	23	58.4	44	111.8
4	102	10.2	24	61.0	45	114.3
4½	114	11.4	25	63.5	46	116.8
5	127	12.7	26	66.0	47	119.4
6	152	15.2	27	68.6	48	121.9
7	178	17.8	28	71.1	49	124.5
8	203	20.3	29	73.7	50	127.0

yards to metres

yards	metres	yards	metres	yards	metres	yards	metres	yards	metres
⅛	0.11	2⅛	1.94	4⅛	3.77	6⅛	5.60	8⅛	7.43
¼	0.23	2¼	2.06	4¼	3.89	6¼	5.72	8¼	7.54
⅜	0.34	2⅜	2.17	4⅜	4.00	6⅜	5.83	8⅜	7.66
½	0.46	2½	2.29	4½	4.11	6½	5.94	8½	7.77
⅝	0.57	2⅝	2.40	4⅝	4.23	6⅝	6.06	8⅝	7.89
¾	0.69	2¾	2.51	4¾	4.34	6¾	6.17	8¾	8.00
⅞	0.80	2⅞	2.63	4⅞	4.46	6⅞	6.29	8⅞	8.12
1	0.91	3	2.74	5	4.57	7	6.40	9	8.23
1⅛	1.03	3⅛	2.86	5⅛	4.69	7⅛	6.52	9⅛	8.34
1¼	1.14	3¼	2.97	5¼	4.80	7¼	6.63	9¼	8.46
1⅜	1.26	3⅜	3.09	5⅜	4.91	7⅜	6.74	9⅜	8.57
1½	1.37	3½	3.20	5½	5.03	7½	6.86	9½	8.69
1⅝	1.49	3⅝	3.31	5⅝	5.14	7⅝	6.97	9⅝	8.80
1¾	1.60	3¾	3.43	5¾	5.26	7¾	7.09	9¾	8.92
1⅞	1.71	3⅞	3.54	5⅞	5.37	7⅞	7.20	9⅞	9.03
2	1.83	4	3.66	6	5.49	8	7.32	10	9.14

Index